THE CREPE is made of the simplest ingredients—eggs, milk and flour, but it can become the most elegant of entrees and desserts.

THE CREPE is what this flexible, thin pancake is called in France, but there are wonderful French, Italian, Russian, Spanish and Chinese versions.

THE CREPE is supremely adaptable. It performs hot or cold, small or large, as appetizer, main dish, in the soup, as the vegetable course and as the most delectable of desserts.

THE CREPE is the speciality of fine restaurants, but it can be made with a flair by the youngest of cooks.

THE CREPE has manufacturers from all over the country rushing to the market with new equipment, pans of varied shapes and forms for preparation and cooking.

THE CREPE COOKBOOK tells you all you need to know to make **THE CREPE** perfectly, professionally and in 200 different ways. It tells you what pans are best, the simplest ways to make the prize pancake (and illustrates each step), how to deep-fry, shred, wrap, stack, bake, crunch or serve them in flaming splendor.

THE CREPE can be your culinary masterpiece…with the expert advice of the Editors of Consumers Guide® in **THE CREPE COOKBOOK.**

THE
CREPE
COOKBOOK

The Easy Way
to Elegant Crepes

By The Editors of
Consumer Guide®

WARNER BOOKS

A Warner Communications Company

Contents

Photo and Recipe Credits
Credit goes to the following companies and associations for
providing various recipes and/or photos: Alaska King Crab
Marketing and Quality Control Board; California Apricot
Advisory Board; California Raisin Advisory Board; Dole
Bananas; Ekco Housewares Company; Florida Citrus Commis-
sion; John Morrell & Company; National Cherry Growers and
Industry Foundation; National Livestock and Meat Board;
National Peanut Council; Norwegian Canning Industry;
Oster Corporation; Pacific Coast Canned Pears Service; The
Quaker Oats Company; Theodore R. Sills, Inc.; Sterno Canned
Fuel; and the Washington State Apple Commission.

The Versatile Crepe

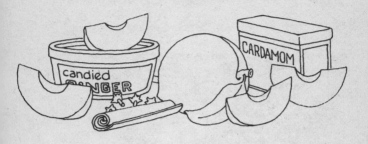

What wraps around, folds over, flames, freezes and generally delights diners all across the country? The crepe, that's what.

It would be hard to think of many foods more versatile than the crepe. Really nothing more than a very thin, very tender pancake, a crepe can embrace almost any combination of ingredients, and can take on an incredible assortment of flavors right in its batter.

Crepe is a French word, and is written *crêpe*. But it has become so popular in America, with creperies, Magic Pan restaurants and crepe pans galore, that its name has become Americanized, too. The French pronounce it Krep, as in step. Americans seem to prefer to rhyme it with tape or shape.

For years the crepe has been kept in the ivory tower of elegant French restaurants, presented only to the most sophisticated diner as Crepes Suzette. But such a good thing could not remain away from the family dining table forever! Although still thought of as elegant,

American consumers are realizing how adaptable the crepe can be—as a container for hundreds of fillings (including leftovers); as the menu star at any imaginable meal or snack; as a party entree that can be fixed ahead and kept on hand.

The crepe is, very simply, a skinny pancake. Typical pancakes are leavened and slightly thick, with a porous texture. Crepes have more eggs and liquid, less flour than pancakes and no leavening. The result is a flat, pliable but tender cake that you can wrap or fold.

Raspberry Blintzes

Making Batters

Crepe-making is not at all difficult. You just mix eggs, milk, flour, some melted butter or oil and salt. Our batter recipes on the following pages give you variation after variation on the basic theme, so you can come up with a flavored batter to complement almost any of the many fillings that follow. If you have a blender, let it mix the crepe batter in one simple step. Or, you can beat the eggs and liquid ingredients with a whip, fork, rotary or electric beater, then add the flour and other dry ingredients and beat until smooth.

Most batters should stand or "rest" for about an hour after mixing and before baking. This resting gets rid of any air bubbles you may have beaten in, and it also gives the flour a chance to absorb some of the liquid. Be sure to stir the batter before using, since it may separate slightly. You may also need to add another tablespoon or two of milk, since the batter may have thickened somewhat. Most batters should be the consistency of cream.

If it will be more than an hour between mixing and baking, cover the batter tightly and refrigerate it. But, let it have some time at room temperature to warm up before baking. The amount of batter needed for a recipe will vary, depending on the size and style of pan you use. Extra batter can be baked and the crepes frozen for future use. In general, if you have a 7- to 9-inch inside-baking pan, start with ¼ cup of batter per crepe and adjust the amount. For 5- to 6-inch pans start with 2 to 3 tablespoons and adjust the amount.

Basic Crepes I

This rich batter should be the consistency of cream. It can be covered tightly and stored in the refrigerator for several days, or even frozen for a week or two. Be sure to let frozen batter thaw in the refrigerator — it will take overnight plus most of a day. Beat well before baking. This batter makes about 3 cups of batter. You can easily double it to make a lot of crepes at one time, if you wish.

    3   eggs
    1½ cups milk
    3   tablespoons butter, melted
    1   cup all-purpose flour
    ½   teaspoon salt

Combine all the ingredients in a blender and blend until smooth. Or, beat the eggs, milk and butter together, then add the flour and salt and beat with a rotary or electric mix until smooth. Let the batter stand about 1 hour before baking.

Basic Crepes II

Some cooks feel that half milk and half water make a more tender crepe than all milk, as in Crepes I. The choice is yours. This batter makes about 2½ cups of batter.

3 eggs
½ cup milk
½ cup water
3 tablespoons butter, melted
¾ cup all-purpose flour
½ teaspoon salt

Combine all the ingredients in a blender and blend until smooth. Or, beat the eggs, then beat in the milk, water and butter. Add the flour and salt and beat until smooth. Let the batter stand for 30 minutes or so, if you have the time. If not, you can bake this batter right away.

Buttermilk Crepes

The tangy tartness of buttermilk adds an interesting flavor. Try these crepes with fruit fillings, cheese or seafood. The recipe makes about 3 cups of batter.

3 to 4 eggs
1 cup buttermilk
½ cup water
3 tablespoons oil
1 cup all-purpose flour
½ teaspoon baking soda
1 teaspoon sugar
½ teaspoon salt

Combine all the ingredients in a blender and blend until smooth. Or, beat the eggs, buttermilk, water and oil together. Add the flour, soda, sugar and salt and beat until smooth. Let the batter stand about ½ hour before baking.

Chocolate Crepes

Rich in chocolate color and flavor, you can use these crepes in any dessert recipe of your choosing, or just fill them with vanilla, mint, chocolate or coffee ice cream and pour on fudge sauce, creme de menthe or other liqueur—superb! The recipe makes about 2 cups of batter. The number of crepes you will get from this recipe depends, of course, on the size and type of pan you use.

    4 eggs
    1 cup half and half
    ¾ cup flour
    ¼ cup regular cocoa
    ¼ cup butter, melted
    2 teaspoons sugar
    1 teaspoon vanilla

Combine all the ingredients and beat well with a rotary or electric beater, or blend the ingredients in a blender until smooth. Cover and let stand ½ to 1 hour before baking. The crepe batter may be prepared several days in advance, but it must be kept covered in the refrigerator until about 1 hour before ready to bake.

Cornmeal Crepes

This batter is a nice complement to hearty meat or cheese fillings and is especially good deep-fried. You must stir the batter before pouring out or dipping each crepe, so the cornmeal stays distributed throughout. The recipe makes about 2 cups of batter and can be doubled.

3 eggs
1 cup milk (or ½ cup milk, ½ cup water)
2 tablespoons oil or butter, melted
¾ cup all-purpose flour
½ cup cornmeal (yellow or white)
¼ teaspoon salt

Combine all the ingredients in a blender and blend until smooth. Or, beat the eggs, then beat in the milk and oil or butter. Add the flour, cornmeal and salt and beat until smooth. Let the batter stand, if you wish, or use it immediately, stirring before each crepe is baked.

Dessert Crepes

Sweet, rich and fruity. These crepes work well in any dessert recipe. You will have about 2 cups of batter.

3   egg yolks
⅔   cup milk
⅔   cup cold water
3   tablespoons cognac
⅓   cup butter, melted
1½ cups all-purpose flour
1   tablespoon sugar
1   teaspoon grated lemon peel
1   teaspoon grated orange peel

Combine all the ingredients in a blender and blend until smooth. Or, beat the egg yolks, milk, water, cognac and butter together. Add the flour, sugar and citrus peels and beat until smooth. Let the batter stand at least 1 hour before baking.

Oatmeal Crepes

Instant oatmeal adds extra flavor and an interesting texture to crepe batter. We like Oatmeal Crepes with tuna, beef and cheese fillings. The recipe makes about 2½ cups of batter.

    3 eggs
    ¾ cup water
    ½ cup milk
    2 tablespoons oil
    ¾ cup all-purpose flour
    1 packet instant oatmeal
    ½ teaspoon salt

Combine all the ingredients in a blender and blend until smooth. Or, beat the eggs, water, milk and oil, then add the flour, oatmeal and salt and beat until smooth. Let the batter stand about 1 hour before baking. Stir the batter frequently while baking crepes.

Orange Crepes

Try this tasty crepe batter recipe with any fruit filling, or with curried shrimp, crab or meat. This crepe batter makes great blintzes, too. The recipe makes about 1¾ cups of batter and can easily be doubled, if you want to bake some crepes to freeze.

3 eggs
2 egg yolks
1 teaspoon grated orange peel
½ cup orange juice
½ cup milk
2 tablespoons butter, melted or oil
1 cup all-purpose flour
1 tablespoon sugar
¾ teaspoon salt

Combine all the ingredients in a blender and blend until smooth. Or, beat the eggs and yolks with orange peel, juice, milk and oil. Add the flour, sugar and salt and beat until smooth. Let the batter stand at room temperature at least 1 hour.

Pancake Mix Crepes

Get a head start on crepe batter with a mix. Because leavening is a part of the mix, these crepes may be just a little plumper than other crepes. The recipe makes about 2 cups batter.

3 eggs
½ cup milk
½ cup pancake mix

Combine all the ingredients in a blender and blend until smooth. Or, beat the eggs and milk together, than add the pancake mix and beat until smooth. You may bake this batter without a standing period.

Parmesan Crepes

These crepes get extra richness and tang from the grated cheese. They are especially nice with cheese and fish fillings. The recipe makes about 3 cups of batter.

    3   to 4 eggs
    1½ cups milk
    3   tablespoons oil
    1   cup all-purpose flour
    ¼   cup grated Parmesan cheese
    ½   teaspoon salt

Combine all the ingredients in a blender and blend until smooth. Or, beat the eggs, milk and oil, then add the flour, cheese and salt and beat until smooth. Stir the batter frequently. Let the batter stand 30 minutes to 1 hour before baking, or bake right after mixing.

Vanilla Crepes

We especially like this batter for dessert crepes. It can be made ahead or can be used immediately. This recipe makes about 2 cups of batter.

3 eggs
¾ cup milk or half and half
1 to 2 tablespoons butter, melted
1 teaspoon pure vanilla extract
¾ cup all-purpose flour
2 teaspoons sugar
¼ teaspoon salt

Combine all the ingredients in a blender and blend until smooth. Or, beat the eggs, milk, butter and vanilla, then add the flour, sugar and salt and beat until smooth.

Whole Wheat Crepes

These crepes are slightly darker in color than Basic Crepes, and with just a little more "chew" to them. Try whole wheat crepes with appetizer, cheese, meat or fish fillings. Remember that you must stir the batter between each crepe baking, otherwise the whole wheat flour will sink to the bottom of the batter. This recipe makes 3 cups of batter.

4 eggs
¾ cup milk
¾ cup water
2 tablespoons oil or butter, melted
1 cup whole wheat flour
1 tablespoon plain or toasted wheat germ
½ teaspoon salt

Combine all the ingredients in a blender and blend until smooth. Or, beat the eggs, then beat in the milk, water and oil. Add the flour, wheat germ and salt and beat until smooth. Let the batter stand about 1 hour before baking. Stir the batter often during baking.

Baking Crepes

Baking crepes is a simple procedure. It does take confidence and a little practice, but once you have made three or four, or perhaps a few more, you will pick up the easy tricks of pouring the batter, tilting the pan and loosening the edges of the crepe to get it out or off. Our step-by-step photos show you how. The instructions that come with your pan should help, too.

Temperature

Too hot or too cold temperatures will not work when it comes to crepe-baking. The pan's temperature must be just right. Medium-high settings seem to be a good starting point for most pans and ranges, but you will have to adjust the heat up or down from that setting depending on your pan, your range and the batter used.

The simplest test for temperature is to sprinkle a few drops of water in or on the pan. If the water immediately vaporizes, the pan is too hot. If the water just sits, the pan is too cold. But if the water droplets dance and skitter around the pan the temperature is just right.

Electric crepe makers present few problems when it comes to temperature because they either maintain just the right temperature or have a thermostatic control that can be set.

Do not be afraid of a little trial and error when it

comes to your first round of crepe making. A few imperfect crepes are no big loss. In fact, even most experts consider the first crepe of each batch to be a test run. Save the first test crepe for Crepe Crisps, or recipes that use less-than perfect crepes.

Baking on the Bottom of the Pan

If a bottom-baking pan is too hot, the crepe will partially cook just as soon as it touches the pan, but will fall off into the plate or dish or batter. If you hold an electric bottom-baking pan in batter too long it will cook the surface of the batter but not stick to the pan. A quick dip in the batter, tilting the pan all around slightly to be sure the entire bottom is coated, is all that you need.

Crepes that bake on the bottom of the pan usually only need to be loosened around the edges. The crepes just drop right off when the pan is inverted. Occasionally you may need to peel off the crepe.

Baking Inside the Pan

Baking crepes inside the pan requires just a little more skill than bottom-baked crepes. You need to judge precisely how much batter is needed to completely cover the bottom of the pan, and not a teaspoon more. That amount, of course, depends on the size of the pan. If your pan is large (7- to 9-inches in diameter across the bottom) set out a ¼ cup measure and start with the measure full of batter. You can then use a scant cup, if necessary, or go up to a ⅓ cup measure for a 9-inch pan. Smaller pans (5- to 6-inches in diameter) usually take 2 to 3 tablespoons of batter. A scant ¼ cup, a small ladle or a coffee measure (2 tablespoons) usually works well for small pans.

Pouring the Batter

When the pan is hot enough to sizzle a drop of water,

quickly pour in the batter and tip and tilt the pan so the batter can completely cover the inside. If, after the inside is covered, there is still some batter moving about on the surface, pour it off into a cup or bowl and use less the next time. If you did not use enough batter you can spoon a little into the uncovered area to patch it. If the pan is too hot the batter will not spread well, and if it is too cold it will spread but not brown.

Turning

Whether you turn crepes and cook them on both sides or not is up to you. Since most crepes are filled you do not have to cook both sides — just put the filling on the unbrowned side. For blintzes you do just the opposite — put the filling on the browned side so that, when you cook the blintzes in butter, the unbrowned side gets the butter treatment.

Removing from the Pan

Depending, of course, on the pan you use, a small spatula, pancake turner and nimble fingers are usually all you need to get crepes out of inside-baking pans. Loosen the edges of the crepe all around with the spatula, then lift up an edge. Use either your fingers or a pancake turner to lift up the crepe. Lift it up and out or just turn the crepe out of the pan.

Storing Crepes

After each crepe is baked, turn it out onto a waxed paper or plastic wrap-covered baking sheet or tray. When you have a single layer of crepes done, cover them with another sheet of paper or plastic wrap and begin another layer of crepes. Some cooks like to tear off squares of waxed paper or plastic wrap and stack the crepes with a paper in between each.

If you are going to fill and serve the crepes right away,

just stack them, as they are baked, in a pie plate or other container, and cover them with a pan lid or piece of foil, to keep them warm and prevent them from drying out. You may also keep the covered container in a low oven to keep the crepes hot.

Preparing in Advance

One of the nicest things about crepes, and crepe batter, is that you do not need to prepare them at the last minute. You can mix up the batter when it is convenient, then cover it tightly and let it wait in the refrigerator until about an hour before you are ready to bake the crepes. Do let the batter stand at room temperature for an hour before baking so it can come to room temperature. Or, if you have some free time, make up a batch, or two, or three of batter, bake the crepes, let them cool and then wrap tightly and freeze. They will keep for several weeks, even a month or two.

To Freeze Crepes

Stack baked crepes with plastic wrap or waxed paper in between, then slip them into a heavy-duty plastic bag, press out all the air and seal tightly. Or, wrap the stack tightly in plastic wrap or aluminum foil and be sure to seal. Do not forget to label the package with the number and type of crepes and the date. Put the crepes in a flat, protected place in the freezer.

To Thaw Crepes

Let the crepes thaw in the unopened package several hours at room temperature or overnight in the refrigerator. If you have a microwave oven, let the crepes thaw there for just a minute or two.

You can also freeze crepe batter, although thawing takes so long it is often easier to whip up a batch of batter than to wait. To freeze batter, pour it into a container and leave at least 1½ inch of head space at the top, so batter can expand as it freezes. Cover tightly, label and freeze. Frozen batter must be thawed in the refrigerator. It will take at least overnight and perhaps part of the next day, so plan accordingly.

Filling Crepes in Advance

It is easy to fill crepes ahead, so that all you have to do at dinnertime or party time is pop them in the oven. Many of the main dish crepes can be assembled and arranged in baking dishes or pans, covered tightly and refrigerated several hours or overnight. Be sure to uncover the pan before baking and add another 5 to 10 minutes to the baking time.

Baking Inside the Pan

Step 1. When water drops dance in pan, the temperature is right. Be sure to add just the right amount of batter.

CONSUMER GUIDE

Step 2. Tip and tilt the pan to spread the batter in a thin, even layer. You will have to work quickly.

Step 3. When crepe is brown on bottom, gently lift the edges to loosen it. Usually, only one side is browned.

CONSUMER GUIDE

Baking on the Bottom of the Pan

Step 1. When water drops dance in pan, the temperature is right. Dip the pan's bottom in the batter for a moment.

Step 2. Return pan to heat; if electric, just turn pan over.
Batter is done when brown on edges and does not look wet.

Step 3. When done, turn pan over and loosen edges. Crepe
should slide off easily. If it sticks, loosen with a spatula.

Folding Crepes

How you fold a crepe depends on what you intend to put in it and whatever fold strikes your fancy. When you begin to manipulate crepes, you may even come up with some unique folds of your own.

The Fold Over is a simple fold that leaves the ends open to show off the filling. The Single Fold is good for fillings that do not have too much sauce, since all you do is tuck the food inside the half-moon crepe. The Quarter Fold is another quick fold, often used for sauced dessert crepes—especially those that are flamed—like Crepe Suzettes. You usually dip whole crepes in a syrup or sauce, then fold them into quarters right in the finishing pan.

There are two versions of the Cornucopia Fold, one that uses whole crepes and one that uses halved crepes. The Cornucopia Fold is particularly good for cheesecake, soufflé or gelatin-based dessert fillings since it shows off the fillings and has such a pretty shape.

Rolling crepes is another easy way to present them. The Simple Roll leaves the ends open and is loose. The Tight Roll is good for fillings that are easily spread and contain small pieces of food, such as some cold appetizer cheese fillings. Just spread the filling over the entire crepe and roll it up tightly. Chill before you cut the roll into bite-sized, pinwheel slices.

The Pocket Roll and the Blintz Fold keep the filling

contained. The Blintz Fold creates a little square packet to be browned in butter. The Pocket Roll makes a slightly rounder filled crepe.

The Crepe Quiche and the Layer or Stack are two unexpected crepe shapes. Crepe Quiches are cuplets made by easing small crepes into muffin pans. Use crepes that have no holes, or the filling will leak through and make it very hard to remove them from the muffin pan. If you can make only large crepes, you can trim off about an inch all the way around so the crepes will not flop out of the muffin cups.

Layered or Stacked Crepes make an impressive arrangement. You can put almost any filling that spreads well on whole crepes, then layer them as high as you like. If you use a dessert filling you are entitled to call your layered creation a "gateau" or cake.

Fold Over

Step 1. Spread or spoon the filling down the center of the unbrowned side of crepe. Raisin Apple Crepes are shown.

Step 2. Fold one side almost all the way across the filling. The filling should show at the ends.

Step 3. Bring the opposite side across the first fold so it overlaps enough to stay in place.

CONSUMER GUIDE

Single Fold

Step 1. Place the crepe's best side down. Arrange filling on half the crepe and fold the other side over.

Step 2. Ham and Asparagus Crepes are ready for the baking pan. Mornay Sauce is poured over them before baking.

Quarter Fold

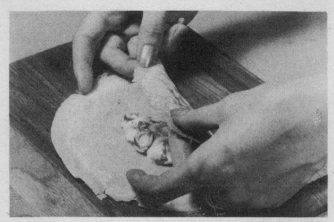

Step 1. Put crepes brown-side down, spoon filling in center and fold in half. Puffy Cheese Olive Crepes are shown.

Step 2. Fold in half again. The Quarter Fold is sometimes not filled, as for Crepe Suzettes.

Halved Crepes

Step 1. Place filling in the center of half a crepe. Tropical Crepes made with candied fruit are shown.

Step 2. Fold 1/3 of the half-circle just over the filling; roll up the crepe to form a cornucopia.

Cornucopia Fold

Step 1. Put the best side of the crepe down. To show off fillings, first place filling on a third of the crepe.

Step 2. Fold a third of the crepe part way over the filling. These are Lemon Yogurt and Strawberry Crepes.

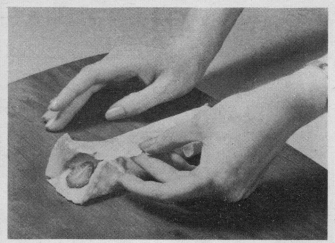

Step 3. Fold the opposite third of the crepe so it overlaps the first fold, forming a triangle with the filling showing.

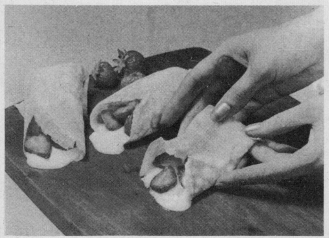

Step 4. Tuck the point of the triangle under the crepe to hold the cornucopia in shape.

Simple Roll

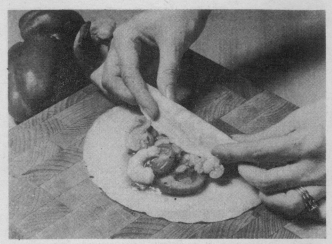

Step 1. Place browned side down. Spoon filling in center. Fold 1/4 of the crepe over part of the filling.

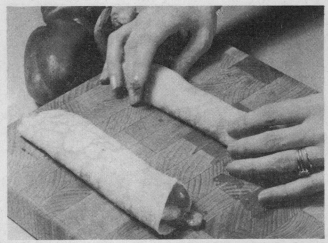

Step 2. Start rolling up the crepe from the folded edge. Sweet and Sour Shrimp Crepes are shown.

Tight Roll

Step 1. Place the prettiest side down. Spread the filling almost to the edge of the crepe.

Step 2. Roll the crepe up tightly like a jelly roll. Here, Nutty Bleu Cheese Crepes are being rolled up.

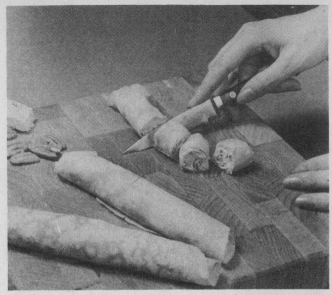

Step 3. For bite-sized appetizers, cut the rolled crepes into small cross-sections and arrange them on a serving platter.

Pocket Roll

Step 1. Put the crepe's best side down. Spread the filling in the center. Chocolate Orange Mousse Crepes are shown.

CONSUMER GUIDE

Step 2. Fold the opposite sides to cover a little of the filling, leaving some filling showing in the center.

Step 3. Start rolling up the crepe and include the folded sides as you roll.

Step 4. Crepes are arranged seam-side down and garnished with whipped cream, orange peel and chocolate shavings.

Blintz Fold

Step 1. If you are deep-frying blintzes, fill the browned side. Otherwise, spread filling in the center as shown.

Step 2. Bring one side up to cover half the filling. Lemon Blintzes are being folded here.

Step 3. Bring the right and left sides up to slightly overlap each other. Be sure to include the first fold.

Step 4. Roll the crepe over to complete the fold. The seam side will be on the bottom.

Crepe Quiche

Crepe Quiche. Use small crepes, best side up, or cut large ones to fit in greased muffin tin cups. Fill.

Layer or Stack

Step 1. Spread the best side of each crepe with filling. Peanut Gateau is being assembled here.

Step 2. Stack the spread layers one on top of the other. Work quickly if the filling tends to melt.

Step 3. Decorate the top, if desired. Then, cut in wedges to serve. Whipped cream and peanuts are added here.

Crepe Pan Test Reports

Crepe pans come in 4 styles: inside-bakers (skillets), bottom-bakers, electric pans, and finishing pans.

Inside-Bakers (skillets)

The traditional crepe baking pan is a slope-sided skillet that bakes inside; it is often used for omelets or to saute' other foods. It may be 5 to 8 or 9 inches across the bottom, made of enamel over iron, aluminum, steel, even cast iron. Sloping sides are an important feature, so you can slip a spatula down the side to loosen the crepe edge for easier removal and turning. Choice of plain or non-stick finish is up to you, but Teflon or other non-stick finishes can simplify cleaning up. Crepes baked in these pans are slightly thicker than those baked on the outside or bottom of pans.

Bottom-Bakers

The latest fashion in crepe pans is bottom-bakers. These pans look as if they were made upside down. They are dome-shaped. You dip the bottom of the heated pan into the batter, then invert the pan over the heating element of your range to bake. Crepes from these pans are very thin and you usually get more crepes per cup of batter than with inside-bakers.

Electric Pans

The newest crepe pans are electric, with thermostatic controls. Several are available now and more will be appearing. These pans are expensive, but turn out perfectly browned crepes every time. Most of them are bottom-bakers, one is a small skillet that bakes inside and can be used as you would any small electric skillet.

Finishing or Crepes Suzette Pans

These pans are often large, 10 or 12 inches in diameter, and always shallow. They are not used for baking crepes, but for preparing and presenting them at the table. The top pan, or blazer pan, of a chafing dish falls into this category, too. These finishing pans are often copper, with tin linings, and are always expensive. They do add an elegant touch to table-side preparation, but are not necessary for most of the recipes in this book.

Pan Sizes

Most crepe pans fall into 2 size ranges: small, producing crepes about 5 to 6 inches in diameter; and large, creating crepes about 8 inches across. Many of our recipes call for a certain number of large and twice as many small crepes. Some just say "6 crepes" because we know the amount of filling will fit in either size.

Should you begin creating your own filling recipes, plan on about 2 to 3 tablespoons filling in small crepes, ¼ to ⅓ cup in each large crepe.

Small crepe pans usually require 2 to 3 tablespoons of batter for each crepe, large pans take 3 to 4 tablespoons of batter.

Always read and follow the directions that come with your pan. Always prepare and season the pan following package or use and care instructions. Clean the pan and store it following those instructions, too.

Inside-Baker Crepe Pans

Atlas Metal Spinning 7-inch Skillet

Atlas Metal Spinning Co.
183 Beacon St.
So. San Francisco, CA 94080

This rolled steel skillet with a wooden handle requires

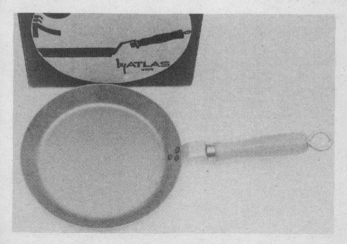

Atlas Metal Spinning 7-inch Skillet

long seasoning, but once seasoned, it works fairly well for small skillet jobs. The handle is heavy and difficult to control and we had a problem with hot spots. It did come with a small recipe folder and use and care information. Because of the hot spots we do not recommend it for crepes.

Approximate retail price: $9.50

Copco 6-inch Skillet

**Copco
111 E. 26th St.
New York, NY 10010**

These well-known pans are enamel on cast iron. They are attractive and heat evenly. The small skillet makes a 5½-inch crepe and would be nice for other small cooking jobs. But, for a lot of crepes, the pan is just too heavy to work with, and the handle becomes quite warm. Al-

Copco 6-inch Skillet

CONSUMER GUIDE

though beautifully designed and easy to clean, we think it would be better for frying eggs or sautéing than for crepes. For a little pan, it is also expensive.

Approximate retail price: $9.50

Gourmet Limited Crepe Suzette Pan

Gourmet Limited
376 E. St. Charles Rd.
Lombard, IL 60148

This beautiful polished aluminum skillet is a shallow inside-baker, with just a slight edge. It makes attractive 7-inch crepes, has a cool, wooden handle with a hole to hang it up, is not too heavy to work with, and is altogether satisfactory, but also quite expensive. We think other, less-expensive pans work just as well, even though they may not be as attractive. The pan comes with a leaflet including seasoning and basic crepe-making instructions.

Approximate retail price: $23.00

Gourmet Limited Crepe Suzette Pan

La Crêpe Complete

La Crêpe Complete

Hoover
North Canton, OH 44720

This non-stick coated electric skillet makes large, 7½-inch crepes that are beautifully browned because the temperature is thermostatically controlled. The crepe pan is really an electric skillet with a detachable control and has many other uses in addition to crepes. The pan comes with a ¼ cup measure for easy batter pouring. The cord also has a handy clip to hold it to a table leg, so you can use it at the table and not worry about someone tripping over the cord and pulling the pan off the table. Because the sides of the pan are straight up and down, rather then sloping, it is not quite as easy to get the crepes out, but the thermostatic control is of considerable benefit, especially if your range is not easy to control. The instructions and recipe booklet are attractive and very complete. We like the pan very much but it is expensive.

Approximate retail price: $29.95

Metal Skillet from France

Hoan Products (Importer)
615 E. Crescent Ave.
Ramsey, NJ 07446

This heavy, 5½-inch skillet comes with no label and no instructions, but is found in many better housewares departments and cookware shops. We seasoned it by heating oil in it over very low heat for about an hour; it made satisfactory small crepes. But, the handle is

Metal Skillet from France

Popeil Crepe Magician

metal and does get hot, and the pan is heavy. It is a nice little all-around pan, but it is not inexpensive.
Approximate retail price: $5.50

Popeil Crepe Magician

Popeil Brothers, Inc.
2323 W. Pershing Rd.
Chicago, IL 60609

The Crepe Magician is a nifty little pan, designed especially for crepe making. It bakes small (6-inch) crepes inside the very shallow, Teflon-lined pan. It is easy to pour out excess batter because sides of pan are low; it is also easy to loosen crepes to get them out of the pan. The handle has a metal loop so it can be hung up for storage, and the handle does stay cool. The pan is easy to use, lightweight and inexpensive. It comes with a plastic container and a cover to hold the crepes for refrigerator or freezer storage. The storage container is very light in weight and will not withstand other packages stacked on it in the freezer. We suggest you slip the container inside a plastic bag and seal well, to keep crepes airtight. The accompanying book, *50 Things You Can Do With Crepes,* is very well done, with good illustrations and many, many recipes. Widely advertised and also widely available, we think the Crepe Magician is a Best Buy.

Approximate retail price: $9.95

T-Fal 8½-inch Skillet

T-Fal Housewares
1 Montgomery St.
Belleville, NY 07109

This widely-demonstrated, French-made skillet bakes small, 6½-inch crepes on the inside of the skillet. Baking is fast and even. The sloping sides help you get the

T-Fal 8 1/2-inch Skillet

crepes out easily and also let you pour off excess batter, if necessary. The patented, mechanically-bonded, non-stick finish really works, but will discolor if overheated. The pan is lightweight, easy to handle, and has a metal ring so it can be hung up for storage. The skillet can also be used for omelets or other cooking. T-Fal pans are widely available, relatively inexpensive and have uses other than crepe-baking, so we rate them a Best Buy.

Approximate retail price: $8.99

Toroware Aluminum Skillet by Leyse

Leyse Aluminum Company
Kewaunee, WI 54216

This heavy, aluminum skillet makes 6-inch crepes inside the skillet. After proper seasoning and proper adjustment of temperature, it makes very nice crepes. The handle is metal and does get hot—you will need a pot holder to protect your hands. The sides are sloped so

Toroware Aluminum Skillet by Leyse

West Bend 10-inch Skillet

you can loosen and turn out the crepes fairly easily. It is a moderately expensive, multi-use item.
Approximate retail price: $6.99

West Bend 10-inch Skillet

West Bend Company
400 Washington St.
West Bend, WI 53095

This skillet can be used for any crepe-baking, frying, sautéing and omelets. Its sloping sides and non-stick finish make it a nice crepe baker. It makes large, 8-inch crepes, heats fairly evenly, is lightweight and easy to handle, with a metal ring to hang up for storage. If you are going to bake crepes only occasionally, and want a pan that can do other cooking jobs as well, then this is the one for you. It comes with instruction book and batter measuring cup.
Approximate retail price: $7.99

Bottom-Baker Crepe Pans

Atlas Metal Spinning Crepe Master

Atlas Metal Spinning Co.
183 Beacon St.
So. San Francisco, CA 94080

This bottom-baking pan sits on a metal ring, with air holes all around, which holds it above the burner. The pan requires seasoning and does discolor as a result, but it performed very well and consistently turned out evenly-browned large (about 8-inch) crepes. The Crepe Master comes with an instruction and recipe booklet, has a wooden handle and is easy to use.
Approximate retail price: $15.95

Atlas Metal Spinning Crepe Master

The Crepe Maker by Alfred E. Knobler

The Crepe Maker by Alfred E. Knobler

Alfred E. Knobler & Co. Inc.
Moonachie, NJ 07074

This sturdy, heavy bottom-baking pan with wooden handle looks great, but turned out to be our least favorite. The handle design makes it almost impossible to dip in anything other than a very shallow plate and get batter on the complete surface of the pan to make an 8-inch crepe. Also, the rim at the edge of the pan was a hindrance in removing crepes, rather than a help. The Crepe Maker comes with seasoning instructions and an attractive recipe leaflet that has several recipes and shows folding techniques, but an adequate book cannot overcome inadequate design or performance.
Approximate retail price: $13.95

Ekco Flint Crepes-Plus

Ekco Flint Crepes-Plus

Ekco Housewares Company
9234 W. Belmont
Franklin Park, IL 60131

This stainless steel pan comes in two sizes—7 or 8 inches. You can use it as an inside or outside baker, but we much prefer it as an outside or bottom-baker. It is too hard to get crepes out of the inside of the skillet, although nice to have the skillet for other uses. The Crepes-Plus comes with an attractive and very helpful instruction and recipe book, the pan is easy to use (as a bottom-baker) and performs well (as a bottom-baker). It is not as easy to clean as non-stick coated pans, but still would make a nice gift or multi-use pan for your kitchen. **Approximate retail price: $9.99 (7-inch); $12.95 (8-inch)**

Magik Crepe Pan, Gourmet Limited

Gourmet Limited
376 E. St. Charles Rd.
Lombard, IL 60148

Another beautiful polished aluminum pan from Gourmet Limited, but this one is a bottom-baker. The wooden handle is cool, easy to hold. The pan makes very nice crepes about 7 inches in diameter and is easy to work with. As nicely designed and attractive as its sister Suzette Pan, the Magik Crepe is also expensive. It comes with a small leaflet that gives seasoning and basic crepe-making instructions.
Approximate retail price: $20.00

Grandinetti Electric Crepe Pan

Grandinetti Products, Inc.
2815 Los Flores Blvd.
Lynwood, CA 90262

The first of the electric crepe-makers, the Grandinetti makes beautiful, large (8½-inch), perfectly browned crepes every time. It comes with a plastic spatula and deep plate to hold the batter for dipping. The shape of the plate is just a little too deep, we think, making the last ¼ cup of batter impossible to reach. The only difficulty we had with this crepe maker was an occasional hole forming right in the center of the crepe, which required patching with a drop or two of batter dropped from a spoon. When we held the pan in the batter longer, hoping to eliminate the hole, the batter cooked on its surface and not on the pan. These problems were minor, but we do think the temperature of the handle is a major problem. It gets hot enough during baking that

Magik Crepe Pan, Gourmet Limited

Grandinetti Electric Crepe Pan

you need a pot holder to protect your hand as you dip and turn out the crepes. The Grandinetti has a Teflon coating, an excellent recipe booklet, good use and care instructions, a limited 1-year warranty and UL approval. **Approximate retail price: $29.95**

Nordic Crepe-ette

Nordic Crepe-ette

**Northland Aluminum Products, Inc.
Highway No. 7 and the Beltline
Minneapolis, MN 55416**

This bottom-baking, lightweight, non-stick coated pan comes with a very complete instruction book, many recipes, and a metal pie pan to hold the batter for dipping. It makes 7½-inch crepes, is very easy to use, has a lightweight wooden handle that does not conduct heat. The handle has a thong for hanging. The Nordic pan is well designed for dipping because the handle bridges the batter bowl. This means the entire baking surface of the pan can get down into the batter to make a full-size, even crepe. Proper temperature is important for success with this and all other bottom-baking pans. Crepes come off bottom of pan quite easily. A crepe-only item, but the handle design and handy pan for dipping make this a Best Buy.
Approximate retail price: $9.95

Taylor and NG Crepe Maker

Taylor and NG
650 Howard St.
San Francisco, CA 91045

This bottom-baking pan is high-domed, with holes around the side (for air circulation and even heating, we assume). Proper seasoning is a must for this pan; it comes with seasoning directions and a nice leaflet of recipes although with no specific directions for bottom baking. The handle is wooden, large but easy to work with, and cool. The handle has a ring on the end so you can hang it up. Some may find it heavy to handle. It takes a few crepes to get the hang of it, but otherwise we found it excellent in performance. It makes large (8-inch) crepes. At the price, it is on a par with the Nordic and Popeil and well worth your consideration.
Approximate retail price: $10.49

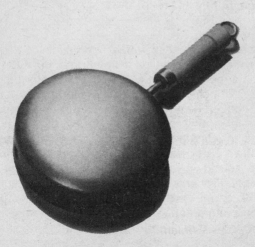

Taylor and NG Crepe Maker

Crepes for Appetizers

Crepes make unusual, delicious appetizers. You can spread them with cheese and nuts, or roll them up to make such taste tempters as Chinese Crab Roll and Lemony Artichoke Appetizers. For a change of shape, try the Viking 24-layer Crepe Stack cut into wedges or Crab Quiche Crepes. Best of all, you can make most of them ahead of time. These appetizers will whet your guests' or family's appetite—for more crepes!

Bleu Cheese and Vegetable Appetizer Crepes

Rich and smooth, these appetizer crepes have the delightful crunch of fresh vegetables. Make them ahead for special parties. The recipe makes 2 dozen small crepes.

- 2 medium carrots, shredded
- 2 stalks celery, finely chopped
- 2 packages (3 ounces each) cream cheese, softened
- 2 ounces bleu cheese
- 1 teaspoon instant minced onion
- ¼ cup chopped pecans
- 24 small crepes

Combine the carrots, celery, cream cheese, bleu cheese, onion and pecans and blend well. Spread about 1 tablespoon over each crepe. Roll up tightly, cover and refrigerate. Serve whole crepes, or cut each in half or thirds to increase number of appetizers.

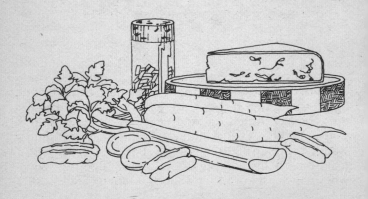

Braunschweiger Cheese Stacks

Pimiento cheese and braunschweiger make hearty little pick-ups that go well with dill pickles and beer. You will have 2 to 4 dozen squares, depending on the size of the crepes.

   ¾ cup braunschweiger
   2 jars (10 ounces each) pimiento cheese spread
  12 crepes

Spread each of 6 crepes with about 2 tablespoons braunschweiger. Spread each of 6 crepes with 2 rounded tablespoons of cheese spread. To make two stacks, 6 crepes high each, alternate 3 each of braunschweiger and cheese spread crepes. Cover and chill for easier slicing. Cut the stacks into 1-inch squares.

Chinese Crab Roll

Shrimp may also be used instead of the crabmeat for a variation on these oriental crepes. The recipe makes 16 appetizers.

  2 *tablespoons chopped green onion*
  2 *tablespoons minced celery*
  2 *teaspoons oil*
  2 *tablespoons finely chopped carrots*
  ½ *cup minced pork or chicken*
  ½ *cup minced crabmeat*
  1 *teaspoon sugar*
  ½ *teaspoon salt*
  ⅛ *teaspoon pepper*
     Oil
16 *small crepes*

Saute' the onions and celery in 2 teaspoons oil until soft. In a medium bowl, combine the onions, celery, carrots, pork and crabmeat; stir in sugar, salt and pepper. Place about 1 tablespoon of filling on each crepe. Fold the crepes like blintzes (see Folding Crepes). Press the seams together with a fork dipped in crepe batter. Chill the rolls. Brown the rolls in hot oil in a skillet over medium heat.

Cottage Cheese Crepes

Try these opulent cheese-filled crepes as an appetizer, a side dish or a light entree. The recipe makes 8 small or 4 large crepes.

- 1 cup cottage cheese
- ½ cup dairy sour cream
- ½ cup grated Parmesan cheese
- 1 tablespoon instant minced onion (optional)
- 1 teaspoon Worcestershire sauce (optional)
- 8 small or 4 large crepes

Combine the cottage cheese, sour cream, Parmesan, onion and Worcestershire sauce and mix well. Spread about 1 generous tablespoon onto each large crepe; spread 1 scant tablespoon on each small crepe. Roll up or fold as for blintzes (see Folding Crepes). Arrange in well-buttered baking dish or pan and heat in a preheated 350°F oven about 10 minutes, or brown in butter in chafing dish, finishing pan or skillet.

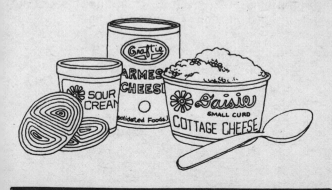

Crab Quiche Crepes

Serving crab in crepes helps make a little go a long way. As with other crepe-quiche recipes, be sure there are no holes in crepes, and use small crepes. The recipe makes 6 entrees or 12 appetizer servings.

> 1 can (7½ ounces) or 1 package (6 ounces) frozen crab
> 12 small crepes
> ¾ cup shredded Swiss cheese
> ¼ cup grated Parmesan cheese
> 2 eggs
> 1 cup half and half
> 2 teaspoons chopped chives
> ¼ teaspoon salt
> ¼ teaspoon Worcestershire sauce
> Dash hot pepper sauce

Drain and slice the canned crab; thaw, drain and slice the frozen crab. Ease the crepes into greased muffin tins. Divide the crab among the crepe-lined tins. Stir the cheeses together and divide among the crepes. Beat the eggs lightly, then beat in the half and half and seasonings. Pour over the crab and cheese. Bake the crepes in a preheated 350°F oven 35 to 40 minutes, or until a knife inserted off-center comes out clean.

Cream Cheese and Lox Crepes

These appetizers have a zippy onion twist. You will get 5 to 6⅔ dozen appetizers from the recipe.

1 package (8 ounces) cream cheese, softened
½ cup grated onion
3 tablespoons lemon juice
½ teaspoon coarsely ground pepper
¼ pound lox
10 crepes

Whip the cream cheese, onion, lemon juice and pepper until smooth. Cut the lox into slivers. Spread about 2 tablespoons of the filling evenly on each crepe, sprinkle with lox. Roll up. Cut into 6 to 8 bite-sized pieces, depending on size of crepe.

Deviled Ham Crepes

This is finger food at its finest—delicious for party trays or a smorgasbord. You'll get about 8 dozen appetizers.

> 1 package (3 ounces) cream cheese, softened
> ⅓ cup mayonnaise
> 1 can (4½ ounces) deviled ham
> 2 tablespoons chopped capers
> 1 tablespoon lemon juice
> 1 teaspoon horseradish
> 12 crepes

In a medium bowl, beat the cream cheese and mayonnaise until smooth. Stir in the remaining ingredients, except the crepes. Chill. Spread 2 tablespoons of the mixture on each crepe. Roll up. Chill. Cut into about 12 bite-size pieces.

Deviled Salmon Stacks

Not only do these wedges of stacked crepes look pretty, but they are delectable. Garnish the wedges with slices of lemon and parsley. The recipe yields 24 appetizers.

  4 eggs, hard-cooked
  1 can (3¾ ounces) salmon
  ¾ cup mayonnaise
  1 tablespoon minced onion
  1 tablespoon lemon juice
  1 tablespoon Worcestershire sauce
  ½ teaspoon seasoned salt
  ½ teaspoon celery salt
16 crepes

Chop the eggs very fine and place them in a medium bowl. Add the remaining ingredients; stir to blend until smooth. Spread about 2 tablespoons of filling over the entire surface of each crepe. Stack one on another to make 4 stacks, each 4 layers high. Press each stack together. Cover and chill. Cut each stack into 6 wedges. Serve plain or with Hollandaise sauce.

Fruit and Sausage Bits

Here are some choice morsels to whet appetites before dinner. The recipe yields about 3 dozen appetizers.

> ¼ cup prepared mustard
> ⅔ cup currant jelly
> 1 tablespoon lemon juice
> ⅛ teaspoon coriander
> 1 cup drained pineapple chunks
> 2 cans (5 ounces each) Vienna sausages
> 7 crepes, cut in half

In a small saucepan, heat the mustard, jelly, lemon juice and coriander, stirring occasionally until smooth. Add the pineapple chunks. Place one sausage on each half crepe. Roll and cut in half. Place the cut crepes in a shallow chafing dish or in a pan on a warming tray. Pour the sauce over them. Serve warm with toothpicks.

Guacamole Crepes

Almost like tacos, Guacamole Crepes are tender instead of crisp. Serve single small crepes as appetizers, larger crepes for luncheon or brunch. The recipe makes 6 brunch or 12 appetizer servings.

   2 medium avocados
   2 to 3 tablespoons lemon juice
   1 tablespoon minced onion
   ½ teaspoon salt
      Dash hot pepper sauce
   6 large or 12 small crepes
   1 medium tomato, chopped or 8 cherry tomatoes, halved
   1 cup shredded lettuce
   ½ cup shredded Cheddar cheese

Peel and pit the avocados. Mash with the lemon juice, onion, salt and pepper sauce. Spread the avocado mixture over the crepes and roll up. Sprinkle with tomato, lettuce and cheese.

Ham and Cheese Crepe Stack

All you have to do for this recipe is open some jars, bake some crepes and spread and stack. This hearty appetizer must be well chilled, so it is a natural to prepare a day ahead of a party. Cover the stack tightly with foil or plastic wrap when it is refrigerated. Cut it into wedges to serve. You will have 24 appetizer wedges.

> 2 cans (4½ ounces each) deviled ham
> 2 jars (8 ounces or 6 ounces each) pasteurized process
>   cheese spread
> 8 large crepes

Spread 4 crepes with the deviled ham; spread 4 crepes with cheese. Stack, alternating ham and cheese layers. Cover it tightly and refrigerate. Cut the stack in wedges to serve.

Herring Surprise Pickups

These will sharpen the appetite — for more. Fortunately, the recipe makes 32 appetizers.

  1 jar (10 ounces) pickled herring
  1 cup dairy sour cream
  ⅓ cup chopped onion
  1 teaspoon dill weed
  ¼ teaspoon pepper
 16 crepes, cut in half
 16 dill pickle slices

Drain the herring; chop. In a medium bowl, stir together the sour cream, onion, dill weed and pepper; fold in the chopped herring. Spread 1 tablespoon herring filling on each half crepe. Place one pickle slice on each crepe. Fold into a triangle.

Lemony Artichoke Appetizers

Perfect for cocktail appetizers, these scrumptious crepe nibbles are dipped in Hollandaise sauce. The recipe yields 4 dozen appetizers.

 1 can (7.5 ounces drained weight) artichoke bottoms
24 crepes, cut in half
    Hollandaise Sauce

Cut each artichoke bottom into 8 triangles. There are usually 6 artichoke bottoms to a can. Place each piece in the center of half a crepe. Spoon 1 teaspoon Hollandaise Sauce on top. Fold the crepe around the artichoke and secure it with a toothpick. To serve, dip the wrapped artichoke bottom in Hollandaise Sauce.

Hollandaise Sauce

 1 cup butter, softened
 6 egg yolks
 ½ teaspoon salt
 ⅛ teaspoon pepper
 ¼ cup lemon juice

In a double boiler, beat the butter until creamy; add the egg yolks, beating until blended. Add the remaining ingredients. Cook over simmering water, stirring constantly, until thickened.

Marinated Hearts of Palm Rolls

When you need a high-class appetizer, try this unusual recipe. It yields 2 dozen appetizers.

1 can (8 ounces) hearts of palm, drained
½ cup Italian dressing
¾ cup mayonnaise
½ cup chopped pimiento-stuffed green olives
12 crepes

Slice the hearts of palm into thin strips. In a shallow dish, marinate them in the Italian dressing for 2 hours or overnight, if possible. Stir together the mayonnaise and olives. Spread 1 tablespoon of mayonnaise on each crepe. Divide the hearts of palm strips evenly on the crepes. Roll up. Slice in half to serve.

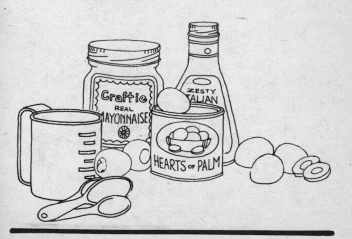

Mustard Sardine Wraps

A delicacy from the sea, these crepes would make an unusual addition to a smorgasbord. The recipe makes 32 appetizers.

6 tablespoons dijon mustard
1 tablespoon lemon juice
1 tablespoon horseradish
2 cans (4 ounces each) sardines in wine sauce, mustard sauce or plain
8 crepes, cut in half

Stir together the mustard, lemon juice and horseradish. Spread about 1½ teaspoons of the mixture on each half crepe. Divide the sardines evenly among the halved crepes. Roll. Cut each roll in half to serve.

Nippy Clam Spirals

A light touch for a party. The flavor improves overnight so be sure to make plenty to have the next day. You will have 6 dozen appetizers with this recipe.

    1 can (6½ ounces) minced clams
    1 package (8 ounces) cream cheese
    2 tablespoons minced onion
    2 tablespoons chopped pimiento
    1 tablespoon lemon juice
    1 teaspoon Worcestershire sauce
      Dash salt
      Dash garlic powder
      Dash cayenne pepper
      Dash hot pepper sauce
    9 crepes

Drain the clams, reserving 4 tablespoons of juice. Whip together all the remaining ingredients, except the crepes. Add 3 to 4 tablespoons clam juice to make the mix smooth enough to spread. Spread about 3 tablespoons filling to the edges of each crepe. Roll. Cut into about 8 bite-sized pieces.

Nutty Bleu Cheese Crepes

These crunchy cheese crepes will disappear fast, so be sure to make plenty. The recipe yields 6 to 8 dozen appetizers.

- 1 package (4 ounces) bleu cheese
- 1 package (3 ounces) cream cheese
- 1 cup chopped walnuts or pecans
- ½ teaspoon Worcestershire sauce
- ½ teaspoon grated onion
- ¼ teaspoon salt
- ⅛ teaspoon marjoram
- ⅛ teaspoon pepper
- 12 crepes

Blend the cheeses together until smooth. Add the remaining ingredients. Spread 2 tablespoons of the filling on each crepe. Roll tightly. Cut into 6 to 8 bite-sized pieces, depending on the size of crepe.

Orange Date Triangles

Sumptuous, sweet and delicious, these triangles can be served as appetizers or party sweets. The recipe makes 32 triangles.

  1 package (8 ounces) cream cheese, softened
  ¼ cup orange juice
  1 teaspoon grated orange peel
  1 cup chopped pecans
  1 package (8 ounces) dates, pitted and chopped
  1 teaspoon minced onion
16 crepes, cut in half

Whip the cream cheese with orange juice and orange peel. Stir in the pecans, dates and onion. Spread about 1 tablespoon of filling on each half crepe. Fold each in thirds to form a triangle.

Parmesan Crepe Crisps

Don't discard those less than perfect crepes! Save them well wrapped in the freezer and when you have several tucked away, deep fry them for snacks or special desserts.

> Crepes (at room temperature)
> Oil
> Parmesan cheese

Cut the crepes in quarters. Heat the oil (about 3 inches deep) in a deep saucepan to 375°F. Add the quartered crepes, a few at a time, and fry just until browned, turning if necessary. Remove them at once and drain on paper towels. Sprinkle the crisps with Parmesan cheese while still hot.

Note: for Dessert Crepe Dippers, fry the crepes as above, but sprinkle them with granulated or confectioner's sugar. Heat preserves or jam with a tablespoon of lemon juice or brandy and dip the crepes in hot sauce.

Peanutty Chutney Swirls

Save these spicy peanut treats to surprise and delight the young and old alike. The recipe makes 8 to 10 dozen appetizers.

  1 package (3 ounces) cream cheese, softened
  ¾ cup chunky peanut butter
  ½ cup chutney, chopped
  ¼ teaspoon Worcestershire sauce
  ¼ teaspoon seasoned salt
  3 to 4 tablespoons sherry or water
16 crepes

In a medium bowl, blend together all the ingredients (except the crepes) until smooth. Use the minimum amount of sherry to begin with, adding more as necessary. Spread about 2 tablespoons of mixture on each crepe. Roll and cut into 6 to 8 bite-sized pieces.

Peanutty Pineapple Crepes

These bright, snappy tidbits will give your party tray a light touch. The recipe makes 4 to 6 dozen appetizers.

    1 can (20 ounces) pineapple spears
    1 package (8 ounces) cream cheese, softened
    1 cup chopped peanuts
    12 crepes

Drain the pineapple, reserving ¼ cup juice. Pat the spears dry with paper towels. Whip the cream cheese and pineapple juice together until smooth. Spread about 1 rounded tablespoon of cream cheese on each crepe. Sprinkle about one tablespoon of peanuts on top. Place one spear in each crepe. Roll. Cut into 4 to 6 pieces, depending on the size of the crepe. Secure with toothpicks.

Puffy Cheese Olive Crepes

Creamy smooth Cheddar cheese plus olives and onions make this crepe recipe a family favorite. You will have 16 appetizers.

    ⅔ cup mayonnaise
    1 cup (4 ounces) shredded Cheddar cheese
    1 tablespoon lemon juice
    ½ cup chopped green onions
    ½ cup sliced ripe olives
   16 crepes

Beat together the mayonnaise, cheese and lemon juice until thoroughly blended. Stir in the onions and olives. Spread 2 tablespoons of mixture on crepes. Fold in half, then fold into triangles. Place the crepes on a greased baking sheet. Cover with foil. Heat in a preheated 375°F oven 10 minutes to melt the cheese.

Sausage Chutney Bites

This is a real people-pleaser—hearty and savory. The recipe will make 4 to 6 dozen appetizers.

    12 link sausages
     ½ cup chutney, chopped
    12 crepes

Fry the sausage until browned and cooked through. Spread 1 scant tablespoon of chutney on each crepe. Place one sausage on each crepe. Roll up. Cut the crepes into 4 to 6 bite-sized pieces, depending on the size of the crepe. Serve warm.

Sherried Avocado Crab Crepes

You treat yourself to a captivating combination of flavors when you create crepes with avocado and crab. The recipe makes 12 appetizer servings or 6 main dish servings.

½ cup chili sauce
¼ cup mayonnaise
2 tablespoons sherry
1 teaspoon lemon juice
⅛ teaspoon hot pepper sauce
1 can (7½ ounces) crabmeat
1 cup avocado, peeled, pitted and diced
12 large or small crepes

In a medium bowl, mix together the chili sauce, mayonnaise, sherry, lemon juice and hot pepper sauce. Chill one hour or more. Stir in the crabmeat and avocado. Place a scant 3 tablespoons of filling in the center of each crepe. Roll up.

Shrimp Paté Appetizers

A great way to make a single can of shrimp serve a crowd. The recipe will yield 8 dozen appetizers.

  ¾ cup mayonnaise
  ¼ cup butter, melted
  1 tablespoon lemon juice
  1 teaspoon Worcestershire sauce
    Dash salt
    Dash pepper
  1 can (4½ ounces) shrimp, drained
  1 cup (4 ounces) shredded Cheddar cheese
 16 crepes

Beat together the mayonnaise, butter, lemon juice, Worcestershire sauce, salt and pepper until smooth. Stir in the shrimp and cheese. Spread about 2 tablespoons of filling on each crepe. Roll tightly. Cover and chill for easier slicing. Slice each crepe into 6 sections.

Smokey Cheese Stacks

The smokey flavor brings memories of outdoor barbecuing days inside. The recipe makes 2 to 4 dozen, depending on size of crepe.

    2 jars (10 ounces each) processed cheese spread
    1 tablespoon liquid smoke
    2 teaspoons Worcestershire sauce
    1 teaspoon salt
    10 crepes

In a medium bowl, beat together the cheese spread, liquid smoke, Worcestershire sauce and salt until smooth. Spread 2 tablespoons on each crepe. Stack one on another to make 2 stacks, each 5 layers high. Cover and chill. Cut into 1-inch squares.

Swiss Leek Crepes

Swiss cheese is known for its delightful hazelnut taste and its sweet flavor, as well as for its holes. These crepes take full advantage of the Swiss cheese flavor. The recipe makes 16 appetizers.

  8 *leeks*
  1 *cup bread crumbs*
  3 *tablespoons butter*
  ½ *teaspoon salt*
  ⅛ *teaspoon pepper*
  ¼ *teaspoon nutmeg*
  1 *cup shredded Swiss cheese*
16 *crepes*

Boil the leeks in salted water to cover until tender; pat dry and chop. Brown the crumbs in butter; add the salt, pepper and nutmeg. Layer about 1 tablespoon crumbs, 1 tablespoon cheese and 2 tablespoons leeks on each crepe; roll up. Place the rolled crepes in greased shallow baking dish or baking sheet. Cover with a lid or foil. Bake in a preheated 400°F oven about 5 minutes or until the cheese is melted.

Toasted Sesame Crepes

Nutty sesame seeds and cream cheese have been a winning team at parties for years. The recipe yields 4 to 5½ dozen appetizers.

1 package (8 ounces) cream cheese, softened
¼ cup soy sauce
8 crepes
½ cup sesame seeds, toasted

Beat the cream cheese with the soy sauce until smooth enough to spread. Spread about 2 tablespoons of the mixture on each crepe. Sprinkle about 1 tablespoon of the sesame seeds over each crepe. Roll. Cut into 6 to 8 pieces.

Tuna Cucumber Appetizers

A refreshing combination that suits summer parties like sunshine. The recipe will yield 8 to 10 dozen appetizers.

  1 package (3 ounces) cream cheese, softened
  ½ cup mayonnaise
  1 can (6½ to 7 ounces) tuna, drained and flaked
  2 teaspoons dried dill weed
  1 teaspoon celery salt
  1 cup chopped, seeded cucumber
 16 crepes

In a medium bowl, blend together the cream cheese and mayonnaise. Beat in the tuna, dill weed and celery salt until smooth. Fold in the cucumber. Spread about 2 tablespoons of filling on each crepe. Roll up. Cover and chill. Cut into 6 to 8 bite-sized pieces, depending on the size of the crepe.

Viking 24-Layer Crepe Stack

Sardines star in the savory filling of this spectacular appetizer. You cut wedges from the stack to serve. The recipe makes 24 appetizer wedges.

 1   *can or jar (4 ounces) pimientos*
 2   *green chili peppers, seeded*
 1   *tablespoon sugar*
 1   *teaspoon salt*
 1   *slice onion*
 1   *can (3¾ ounces) Norwegian sardines packed in oil, drained*
24   *small or 12 large crepes*
 1½ *cups dairy sour cream*
    Watercress

In a blender container, combine the pimientos, peppers, sugar, salt and onion slice and blend until smooth. Pour the mix into a small bowl and add half the sardines. Mix well to crush the sardines. Put one crepe on a serving plate and spread with a thin layer of sour cream. Top with another crepe and a thin layer of sour cream. Repeat, spreading each fourth crepe with the sardine mixture as well as sour cream. Repeat until all crepes have been stacked and spread. Arrange the remaining sardines and watercress on top for garnish. If prepared in advance, cover the stack tightly with plastic wrap and chill. Cut into wedges to serve.

Whipped Cream Cheese and Caviar Appetizers

These sophisticated crepes are a suitable prelude to a formal dinner. The recipe makes 6 to 8 dozen appetizers.

>   1 package (3 ounces) cream cheese, softened
>   1 cup dairy sour cream
>   1 hard-cooked egg, chopped
>   3 tablespoons minced onion
>   1 tablespoon lemon juice
>   1 jar (3½ ounces) caviar
> 12 crepes

Whip the cream cheese and sour cream until smooth. Fold in the egg, onion and lemon juice. Spread 2 tablespoons of the mixture evenly on each crepe. Spread 2 tablespoons caviar on each crepe. Roll tightly and chill. Cut into 6 to 8 bite-sized pieces, depending on the size of the crepe.

Wisconsin Bleu Cheese Crepes

These cheese crepes are unbelievably good as appetizers, or omit the chives and top with fresh fruit for an elegant dessert. The recipe makes 12 appetizers or 6 main dish servings.

   2 pounds cream-style cottage cheese
   4 ounces bleu cheese, crumbled
   1 tablespoon sugar
   2 teaspoons chopped chives
   2 teaspoons brandy or lemon juice
  12 small crepes
   2 tablespoons butter

Beat the cottage cheese, bleu cheese, sugar, chives and brandy together, or blend in a blender until smooth. Spread about ¼ cup cheese mixture on each crepe. Roll up. Melt the butter in a finishing pan or the blazer pan of a chafing dish over canned heat. Brown the crepes. Spoon the remaining cheese mixture over to serve.

Wrapped Smoked Oysters

An elegant addition to any party, these tasty bits are quite easy to prepare. The recipe will give you 20 appetizers.

   1 can (3⅔ ounces) smoked oysters
   10 slices bacon, cut in half
   10 crepes, cut in half

Partially cook the bacon; drain on absorbent paper towel. Wrap each oyster with half a strip of bacon. Place each on half a crepe and roll up. Secure with a toothpick. Place the crepes on a baking sheet or shallow baking pan. Cover with foil. Bake in 400°F oven until heated through, about 5 minutes. Place the rolled crepes on paper towel to drain, if necessary.

Main Dish Crepes with Beef, Veal and Lamb

Crepes with an international flair are found in this section—Crepes Stroganoff, Italian Beef Crepes, Sauerbraten Special and Syrian Lamb Crepes, to name a few. The recipes work magic with leftovers and inexpensive cuts of meat, transforming the commonplace into memorable entrees. They are easy to prepare, as well as easy on the budget.

Arroz con Carne Crepes

Surprise the people who think crepes are only served at dainty repasts with these Spanish rice and meat crepes. This recipe makes enough for a hungry crowd—12 servings.

      1 package (7½ ounces) Spanish rice mix
      2 tablespoons butter
      1 pound ground beef
      1 can (1 pound) stewed tomatoes
     ¼ cup minced onion
     ¼ teaspoon seasoned salt
      1 jar (12 ounces) chili sauce
     24 crepes

In a large skillet, brown the rice in 2 tablespoons butter. Add the ground beef; brown. Spoon off excess fat. Add the stewed tomatoes, onion and salt. Cover; cook over low heat about 15 minutes. Meanwhile, heat the chili sauce. Fill each crepe with ¼ cup of the rice-meat mixture. Roll up or fold. Spoon the chili sauce over the crepes and serve at once. Or, arrange the crepes in a greased baking dish or pan. Refrigerate until dinner time, then heat in a preheated 350°F oven 30 minutes.

Beef Burgundy Crepes with Olives

Pimiento-stuffed olives and red wine create a mellow, flavorful filling for these main-dish crepes. This recipe makes 6 servings of 1 large or 2 small crepes each.

  1 pound lean boneless beef, cut in ½-inch cubes
  2 tablespoons butter
  1 medium onion, chopped
  ½ cup red wine
  ½ cup water
  1 beef bouillon cube
  1 bay leaf
  1 cup sliced pimiento-stuffed green olives
  6 large or 12 small crepes
  ½ cup dairy sour cream

Brown the beef in the butter. Add the onion and cook until tender. Stir in the wine, water, bouillon cube and bay leaf. Cover and simmer about 30 minutes or until the beef is tender. Add the olives and heat through. Remove the bay leaf. Spoon about ¼ cup of the mixture in the center of each large crepe; spoon 2 tablespoons in center of each small crepe. Roll up or fold. Top the crepes with sour cream.

Note: To prepare the crepes ahead, stir the sour cream into the beef mixture along with the olives. Fill, roll up and arrange in a greased baking dish. Cover and refrigerate. When ready to heat them, uncover and bake in a preheated 350°F oven 20 to 25 minutes.

Beef and Sour Cream Crepes

This version of stroganoff uses cooked beef—a clever way to have a roast reappear in elegant dress. The recipe fills 12 large or 24 small crepes.

½ pound fresh mushrooms, sliced
1 cup chopped onion
2 tablespoons butter
⅓ cup cold water
2 tablespoons flour
2 beef bouillon cubes, crushed
⅓ cup boiling water
2 tablespoons catsup
2 tablespoons Worcestershire sauce
1 teaspoon prepared mustard
2 teaspoons salt
⅛ teaspoon pepper
1 quart cubed cooked beef
1 cup dairy sour cream
12 large or 24 small crepes

In a large skillet, cook the mushrooms and onion in the butter until tender. Blend the cold water and flour. Dissolve the bouillon cubes in the boiling water. Blend the boiling mixture with the flour mixture and add them to the skillet. Stir in the catsup, Worcestershire, mustard, salt and pepper and cook and stir over medium heat until thickened. Stir in the beef and heat through. Remove the skillet from the heat; blend in the sour cream. Spoon about ½ cup in center of each large crepe; spoon ¼ cup in the center of each small crepe and roll up or fold. Serve at once. To serve later, arrange the crepes in a greased baking dish or pan and refrigerate. Then bake in a preheated 350°F oven 10 to 15 minutes.

Creamy Cheese Chip Beef Crepes

Richly sauced and flecked with mushrooms, this dried beef specialty makes 6 servings.

      Boiling water
  1 jar (4 ounces) dried beef
  ¼ cup butter
  3 tablespoons flour
  1 cup milk
  1 cup dairy sour cream
  1 cup (4 ounces) shredded Cheddar cheese
  1 can (4 ounces) mushroom stems and pieces
  1 teaspoon Worcestershire sauce
  1 teaspoon salt
 12 crepes

Pour boiling water over the beef in a strainer to rinse off some of the salt. In a medium saucepan, melt the butter; add the flour and cook until frothy. Add the milk and cook and stir over medium-high heat until the mixture comes to a boil and is smooth and thickened. Add the sour cream, cheese, mushrooms, dried beef, Worcestershire sauce and salt. Fill each crepe with about ¼ cup of the mixture. Roll up or fold. To serve, spoon the remaining sauce over the crepes.

Creole Beef Crepes

Perhaps you thought ground beef was too commonplace for crepes, but this recipe proves you wrong. These hearty crepes will make 4 to 6 generous servings of 2 or 3 crepes each.

  1 pound lean ground beef
  1 medium onion, chopped
  1 medium green pepper, chopped
  1 can (8 ounces) tomato sauce
  ½ cup water
  1 bay leaf, crumbled
  ¼ teaspoon thyme
  ¼ teaspoon basil
  1 tablespoon brown sugar
  1 teaspoon salt
     Dash pepper
 12 large crepes
  1 cup shredded Cheddar or American cheese

Brown the beef in a skillet. Add the onion and green pepper and cook until tender. Drain off any excess fat. Stir in the tomato sauce, water and spices along with the brown sugar, salt and pepper. Simmer slowly 20 to 30 minutes. Spoon about ¼ cup of the filling down the center of each crepe. Roll up or fold. Arrange the crepes on a greased baking sheet or in a greased baking dish or pan. Sprinkle with cheese. Bake in a preheated 350°F oven about 20 minutes.

Crepes Stroganoff

The famous beef-mushroom-sour cream combination makes a splendid crepe filling. This recipe makes 8 large or 16 small crepes for 8 servings.

  1 pound lean boneless beef, cut in strips ½ x 3 inches
  1 tablespoon butter
  1 cup water
  1 beef bouillon cube
  1 tablespoon instant minced onion
  ½ teaspoon salt
  2 tablespoons tomato paste
  ½ pound fresh mushrooms, sliced
  2 tablespoons butter
  1 tablespoon lemon juice
  2 tablespoons sherry
  1 cup dairy sour cream
  8 large or 16 small crepes

In a skillet, brown the beef in 1 tablespoon butter. Add the water, bouillon cube, onion, salt and tomato paste. Cover and simmer 20 minutes or until the beef is tender. Uncover and simmer 5 to 10 minutes. In a small skillet, cook the mushrooms in the 2 tablespoons butter until tender. Stir in the lemon juice. Add the mushrooms and sherry to the beef mixture, then stir in the sour cream. Heat through but do not boil. Spoon about ¼ cup of the mixture down the center of each large crepe; spoon 2 tablespoons down the center of each small crepe. Spoon any remaining mixture over the top. Serve at once or arrange the crepes in a buttered baking dish or pan; cover and refrigerate. Uncover; bake in preheated 350°F oven 20 minutes.

Herbed Liver Crepes

Liver lovers will rejoice; liver haters will be pleasantly surprised. Subtle touches of rosemary and marjoram complement white wine in the savory sauce. The recipe makes 6 (2-crepe) servings.

- ¼ cup flour
- 2 teaspoons salt
- ⅛ teaspoon pepper
- 1½ pounds beef liver, sliced ½ inch thick
- 3 tablespoons butter or margarine
- 1 medium onion, chopped
- 1 cup water
- ½ cup white wine
- ⅓ cup raisins
- 2 tablespoons catsup
- ⅓ teaspoon rosemary
- ¼ teaspoon marjoram
- 12 crepes
- 1 cup dairy sour cream
- Chopped chives

Stir together the flour, salt and pepper. Dredge the liver in the seasoned flour. Melt butter, in a large skillet. Add the liver and brown it on both sides. Remove the liver from the pan and set it aside. Add the onion to skillet and cook until tender. Stir in the water, wine, raisins, catsup, rosemary and marjoram; simmer 10 minutes, stirring occasionally. Cut the liver in cubes and stir it into the sauce until hot. Spoon about ½ cup of the filling down the center of each crepe. Roll up or fold. Serve at once topped with a dollop of sour cream and sprinkling of chives.

Italian Beef Crepes

Tiny cubes of beef simmered in a rich, red tomato sauce make a hearty crepe filling. The filling is quite tasty in Cornmeal or Parmesan Crepes. This recipe makes 12 crepes, enough for 6 generous servings of 2 crepes each.

    1 pound lean boneless beef, cut in ½-inch cubes
    1 onion, chopped
    1 medium green pepper, chopped
    1 clove garlic, minced
    2 tablespoons oil
    1 cup water
    1 can (6 ounces) tomato paste
    1 tablespoon chopped parsley
    1 teaspoon basil
    1 teaspoon salt
  12 crepes
    1 cup shredded Mozzarella cheese

In a large skillet, cook the beef, onion, green pepper and garlic in oil until the meat is browned and the vegetables are tender. Stir in the water, tomato paste and seasonings. Cover and simmer about 20 to 30 minutes or until the meat is tender. Spoon about ¼ cup of the filling onto each crepe and roll up or fold. Arrange the crepes on a greased baking sheet or in a greased baking dish or pan. Sprinkle them with the cheese. Bake in a preheated 350°F oven 20 minutes.

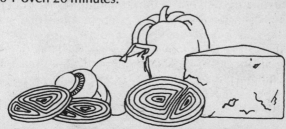

Pepper Steak Crepes

Steak, tomatoes, peppers, onions and spices make a colorful entree for entertaining. The recipe makes 6 (2-crepe) servings, but you could easily double it for a crowd.

1½ pounds sirloin steak
¼ cup oil
1 clove garlic
½ cup chopped onion
1 teaspoon oregano
1 teaspoon salt
½ teaspoon pepper
⅓ cup red wine or beef broth
3 green peppers, seeded and sliced
3 tomatoes, cut into wedges
3 tablespoons cornstarch
2 tablespoons water
12 crepes

Slice meat into 2-inch strips. Brown the meat in the oil in a large saucepan. Stir in the garlic, onion, oregano, salt and pepper, and wine or broth. Cover and simmer until the meat is tender, about 25 minutes. Stir in the green peppers and tomatoes. Mix the cornstarch and water and add it to the meat mixture. Cook, stirring constantly, until thickened. Fill each crepe with ¼ cup of the mixture. Serve with the remaining sauce.

Sauerbraten Special

This quick version of an old German favorite uses ground beef and a special Sauer Sauce. The recipe makes 6 servings.

> 1½ pounds ground beef
> ½ cup chopped onion
> 1 egg
> 1 teaspoon salt
> ⅛ teaspoon pepper
> 2 tablespoons oil
> 6 crepes
> Sauer Sauce

Shape the meat, onions, egg, salt and pepper into six (5-inch) logs. Brown the logs in hot oil until the meat is as done as you like it. Place each log on a crepe. Spoon about 1 tablespoon Sauer Sauce on top. Roll up and put the crepes into a greased, shallow baking dish or pan. Spoon any remaining sauce on top. Bake in a preheated 325°F oven 25 minutes.

Sauer Sauce

> 1 cup water
> 3 tablespoons vinegar
> 3 tablespoons brown sugar
> 2 tablespoons catsup
> 1 tablespoon cornstarch
> 1 teaspoon ground cloves
> ½ teaspoon pepper

Combine all the ingredients in a medium saucepan. Cook, stirring constantly until thickened. Simmer 15 minutes.

Veal a la Marsala

Veal is always something special. For similar flavor but less expense, use chicken or turkey breast, sliced and flattened. The recipe makes 6 (2-crepe) servings.

12 veal cutlets
   Butter
12 slices (1 ounce each) ham
12 slices (½ ounce each) Mozzarella cheese
12 large crepes
   Marsala Sauce

Flatten each veal cutlet by pounding with a mallet or the edge of a plate. Saute' them quickly in butter on both sides. Place one slice ham, one veal cutlet and one slice cheese on each crepe. Roll up the crepes and place them, seam side down, in a shallow baking dish. Pour the Marsala Sauce on top. Bake the crepes in a preheated 375°F oven 10 minutes or until cheese is melted.

Marsala Sauce

⅓ cup sliced green onions
3 tablespoons butter
½ cup Marsala wine
2 teaspoons cornstarch
   Salt
   Pepper

Saute' the green onions in butter until tender. Combine the wine and cornstarch; add them to the butter mixture. Cook and stir until smooth and thickened. Add salt and pepper to taste.

Veal Crepes Paprika

Serve these crepes with a simple green salad, some exotic fresh fruit and a special wine and you will have created a feast. The recipe makes 6 to 8 servings of 2 or 3 large crepes each.

    2 tablespoons butter
    1 pound boneless veal, cubed
    1 medium onion, chopped
    1 tablespoon paprika
    1 tablespoon chopped parsley
    ½ to 1 teaspoon salt
    1 cup water
    2 tablespoons butter
    1 tablespoon lemon juice
    ½ pound fresh mushrooms, sliced
    1 cup dairy sour cream
   12 large crepes

Melt the butter in a skillet. Add the veal and onion and cook until the onion is tender. Add the paprika, parsley, salt and water. Cover and simmer slowly about 30 minutes or until the veal is tender. Meanwhile, cook the mushrooms in 2 tablespoons butter until just tender; stir in the lemon juice. Combine the veal mixture, mushrooms and sour cream. Heat but do not boil. Spoon about ¼ cup of the veal mixture down the center of each crepe and roll up or fold. Serve the crepes immediately or arrange them in a greased baking dish or pan and bake in a preheated 350°F oven 10 to 15 minutes.

Cranberry Lamb Crepes

Lamb cubes simmer in a rich brown sauce with a unique but delightful flavor. You could use beef in place of lamb. The recipe makes 8 large crepes, enough for 4 generous portions or 8 small servings.

- 1 pound lean boneless lamb, cut in ½-inch cubes
- 1 medium onion, chopped
- 2 tablespoons butter or oil
- ⅔ cup water or red wine
- 1 can (8 ounces) strained cranberry sauce
- 1 teaspoon salt
- ¼ teaspoon pepper
- 4 large crepes
- ½ cup dairy sour cream or plain yogurt

Cook the lamb and onion in butter until the lamb is browned and the onion is tender. Add the water or wine, cranberry sauce and seasonings. Cover and simmer 20 to 30 minutes or until the lamb is tender. Spoon about ¼ cup of the filling down the center of each crepe. Roll up or fold. Top each serving with a dollop of sour cream or yogurt.

Greek Crepes

Toasting the pine nuts helps develop their flavor. Pine nuts and a savory blend of spices give the ground lamb a delightful Greek flavor. The recipe makes 8 servings of 2 large or 3 small crepes each.

  1 pound ground lamb
  3 tablespoons olive oil
  2 cups chopped onions
  1 cup cooked rice
  ¼ cup currants
  ¼ cup toasted pine nuts
  1 can (8 ounces) tomato sauce
  ¼ teaspoon ground cinnamon
  ¼ teaspoon ground allspice
  ¼ teaspoon crushed spearmint
  ¼ teaspoon pepper
  1 teaspoon salt
 16 large or 24 small crepes
    Dairy sour cream

In a large skillet, brown the lamb in olive oil. Add the onions and cook until tender. Stir in all the remaining ingredients except the crepes and sour cream. Spoon about 3 to 4 tablespoons of the filling down the center of each large crepe; spoon 1 to 2 tablespoons down the center of each small crepe. Roll up or fold. Arrange them in a greased baking dish. Cover lightly with foil. Bake in a preheated 375°F oven 25 to 30 minutes. Top with sour cream to serve.

Syrian Lamb Crepes

Bring a little foreign flair to the table. Pine nuts, mint, basil, garlic and lamb are just a few of the ingredients in this exotic recipe. You will have 6 (2-crepe) servings.

¼ cup pine nuts
½ cup minced onion
½ clove garlic, minced
2 tablespoons butter
1 pound ground lamb
1 teaspoon dried mint
¼ teaspoon basil
½ teaspoon pepper
½ teaspoon salt
1 can (8 ounces) tomato sauce
12 crepes

In large skillet, brown the pine nuts, onions and garlic in butter. Add the meat, mint, basil, salt and pepper. Brown, stirring often. Add the tomato sauce and simmer 30 minutes. Fill each crepe with about ¼ cup of the meat mixture. Roll up or fold and serve at once.

Main Dish Crepes with Chicken and Turkey

These crepes are worthy of a place of honor at your fanciest brunch, luncheon or dinner. They are quick to fix and refreshingly different from the usual chicken dishes. You will have a hard time deciding which rich, succulent filling to try first.

Baked Chicken and Apple Crepes

Serve this spicy recipe anytime—after the theater, for brunch or dinner. The recipe makes 8 (2-crepe) servings.

     3 cups cubed cooked chicken
     1 can (16 ounces) apple pie filling
    ½ cup chopped pecans
    ½ cup raisins
    ½ cup onions
     1 teaspoon grated lemon peel
    ¼ teaspoon marjoram
    ⅛ teaspoon ground nutmeg
    16 crepes

Combine all the ingredients in a medium saucepan. Heat, stirring occasionally, about 20 minutes. Fill each crepe with about ¼ cup of the mixture. Roll up or fold.

Brandied Chicken

This superb recipe requires a little work, but it is well worth the effort. It makes 6 servings.

- 2 shallots, finely chopped
- ½ pound mushrooms, sliced
- 2 tablespoons butter
- 2 tablespoons brandy
- ½ cup white wine
- 2 tablespoons tomato paste
- 2 chicken bouillon cubes, crushed
- 1 cup boiling water
- 3 cups cooked chicken, cubed
- 12 crepes

Saute' the shallots and mushrooms in the butter until tender. Add the brandy and wine. Simmer until the liquid is reduced by half. Stir in the tomato paste, bouillon cubes and water. Simmer the sauce to reduce it by about ⅓. Add the chicken. Fill each crepe with about ¼ cup of filling. Roll up or fold. Serve immediately.

California Chicken Crepes

You can prepare the crepes and their savory filling ahead, assemble, cover and refrigerate until lunch or dinner time. Add about 10 minutes to the heating time. The recipe makes 4 main-dish servings.

1½ cups dairy sour cream
1½ tablespoons dry onion soup mix
1 teaspoon Worcestershire sauce
1 cup diced cooked chicken
½ cup diced celery
¼ cup finely chopped green pepper
8 large crepes
¼ cup grated Parmesan cheese

Combine the sour cream, soup mix and Worcestershire. Stir in the chicken, celery and green pepper. Spoon about ⅓ cup of the filling down the center of each crepe. Fold or roll the crepes around the filling. Arrange them in a greased baking dish or pan. Spoon any remaining filling over the top. Sprinkle with Parmesan. Bake in a preheated 350°F oven 20 minutes.

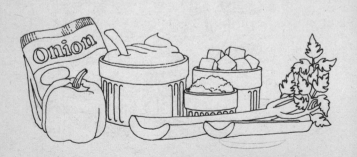

Cashew and Cheddar Chicken Crepes

Smooth and mellow, with the delightful crunch of cashews, these crepes are worthy of a place of honor at your fanciest brunch or luncheon. And they are really quick-to-fix. The recipe makes 12 crepes, for 6 generous servings or 12 single-crepe portions.

> 2 cups cubed cooked chicken (or turkey)
> 1 can (10¾ ounces) cream of chicken soup
> ½ cup shredded Cheddar cheese
> ½ cup cashews
> 1 tablespoon lemon juice
> 1 tablespoon sherry
> 6 large or 12 small crepes

Combine the chicken, soup, cheese, cashews, lemon juice and sherry. Spread ½ cup of the filling over each large crepe; spread a scant ¼ cup of filling over each small crepe. Roll up or fold. Arrange in a greased baking dish or pan and heat in a preheated 350°F oven 15 to 20 minutes.

Chicken Cheese Crepes

You could also try this filling with leftover turkey, ham or tuna. Lemon juice sparks the canned soup in the sauce. The recipe makes 8 servings.

    1 cup diced cooked chicken
    1 cup shredded Swiss cheese
    1 can (10¾ ounces) cream of chicken soup, divided
    ¼ cup chopped green onion or 1 tablespoon instant
       minced onion
    ¼ cup chopped pimiento-stuffed green olives
    8 large or 16 small crepes
    2 tablespoons lemon juice

Combine the chicken, cheese, half the can of soup, onion and olives. Spoon about ¼ cup down the center of each large crepe; spoon 2 tablespoons down the center of each small crepe. Roll up or fold and arrange in a greased baking dish or pan. Stir the lemon juice into the remaining soup and pour over the crepes. Bake in a preheated 350°F oven 20 minutes or until hot and bubbly.

Chicken Crepes Supreme

These crepes are perfect for a company dinner, a brunch, special luncheon or shower. You can use turkey or ham in place of chicken, if you wish. The recipe makes 6 to 8 main-dish servings.

- 3 tablespoons butter
- 2 tablespoons minced onion
- 3 tablespoons flour
- 1 cup milk or chicken stock
- ½ cup half and half
- ¼ cup grated Parmesan cheese
- ½ teaspoon salt
- ¼ teaspoon thyme
- 2 tablespoons butter
- ½ pound fresh mushrooms, sliced
- 1 tablespoon lemon juice
- 2 cups cubed cooked chicken
- 12 large or 24 small crepes

In a medium saucepan, melt the 3 tablespoons butter. Add the onion and cook over medium heat until tender but not brown, about 5 minutes, stirring often. Blend in flour and cook and stir until frothy. Add the milk and half and half; cook and stir until the mixture comes to a boil and is smooth and thickened. Stir in the Parmesan cheese and seasonings. Melt the 2 tablespoons butter in a skillet, add the mushrooms and cook just until tender. Stir in the lemon juice. Combine the sauce, mushroom mixture and chicken and mix. Spoon about ¼ cup of the chicken mixture down the center of each large crepe; spoon about 2 tablespoons down center of each small crepe. Roll up or fold and arrange in a greased baking dish or pan. Pour the remaining chicken mixture over the top. Bake in a preheated 350°F oven about 25 minutes or until hot and bubbly.

Chicken Crepes with Cumberland Sauce

The sweet Cumberland Sauce gives the chicken both color and a tangy flavor. The recipe makes 6 servings of 2 crepes each.

     6 chicken breast halves, boned and skinned
     3 tablespoons butter
        Salt
        Pepper
     6 medium carrots, peeled, cut into julienne strips
    ½ cup chicken broth
     2 tablespoons cornstarch
     1 tablespoon water
    12 crepes
        Cumberland Sauce

Pound the chicken breasts with a mallet or the side of a plate to flatten. Saute' the chicken in the butter just until done. Season with salt and pepper to taste. Cut it into strips and set aside. Add the carrots and broth to the skillet. Simmer until the carrots are crisp tender, about 5 to 8 minutes; remove from the skillet. Blend the cornstarch and water; add them to the liquid in the pan. Cook and stir over medium heat until thickened. Return the carrots and the chicken to the sauce. Divide the mixture evenly among the crepes. Roll up or fold. Place seam side down on a plate. Top with Cumberland Sauce to serve.

Cumberland Sauce

2 tablespoons grated orange peel
½ cup orange juice
2 tablespoons grated lemon peel
¼ cup lemon juice
2 tablespoons cornstarch
2 tablespoons water
1 jar (10 ounces) currant jelly
½ cup Madeira
1 teaspoon dry mustard
½ teaspoon ground ginger
¼ teaspoon salt
1 cinnamon stick

In a small saucepan, combine the peels and citrus juices. Boil slowly for 15 minutes. Blend the cornstarch and water and add to saucepan with all remaining ingredients. Cook and stir over medium heat 20 minutes or until the sauce is reduced to about 1¼ cups. Remove the cinnamon stick.

Chicken Crepes Veronique

The grapes and chicken in this filling are refreshingly different. A tossed green salad or sliced marinated tomatoes and artichoke hearts will complete this menu nicely. The recipe makes 6 (2-crepe) servings.

    3 tablespoons butter
    ¼ cup chopped onion
    1 can (8 ounces) sliced mushrooms, drained
    3 tablespoons flour
    1 cup chicken stock
    ½ cup dry white wine or chicken stock
    ½ teaspoon crushed tarragon
    ½ teaspoon salt
    ¼ teaspoon pepper
    3 whole chicken breasts, cooked and sliced in
      julienne strips
    2 cups halved seedless green grapes
   12 large crepes

Melt the butter in a saucepan. Add the onion and mushrooms and cook until tender. Stir in the flour and cook until frothy. Add the chicken stock, wine, tarragon, salt and pepper. Cook and stir over medium-high heat until the mixture comes to a boil and is smooth and thickened. Combine the chicken, half of the sauce and 1 cup of the green grapes. Spoon about ¼ cup of the filling down the center of each crepe. Fold. Top with the remaining sauce and green grapes. Bake in a preheated 375°F oven 15 to 20 minutes.

Chicken Elegante

Serve this recipe with a grapefruit and avocado salad for a delightful luncheon or supper. The recipe makes 8 (2-crepe) servings.

¼ cup butter
¼ cup flour
2 cups chicken broth
    Salt
    Pepper
1 can (8 ounces) sliced mushrooms, drained
1 can (8½ ounces, drained weight) artichoke hearts, drained, chopped
¾ cup pimiento-stuffed green olives, sliced
3 tablespoons sherry or Madeira
3 cups cubed, cooked chicken
16 crepes

Melt the butter in a large skillet. Add the flour and cook until frothy. Add the chicken broth and cook and stir over medium heat until smooth and thickened. Season to taste with salt and pepper. Stir in the mushrooms, artichoke hearts, olives and sherry. Remove 1 cup of the sauce for topping. Add the chicken to the remaining sauce. Spoon about ¼ cup of the chicken filling down the center of each crepe. Roll up or fold. Serve with the reserved sauce on top.

Chicken or Turkey á la King Crepes

Effortless but exceptional, this recipe is great for the remnants of the holiday bird. The recipe makes 6 (2-crepe) servings.

- ¼ cup chopped green pepper
- ¼ cup chopped onion
- 3 tablespoons butter
- 3 cups cooked cubed chicken or turkey
- 1 can (10¾ ounces) condensed cream of mushroom soup
- 1 can (8 ounces) mushroom stems and pieces, drained
- ½ cup cream
- 1 package (3 ounces) cream cheese, cubed
- 12 large crepes

In a medium saucepan, cook the green pepper and onion in butter until tender. Add the chicken or turkey soup, mushrooms, cream and cream cheese. Cook and stir over medium heat until heated through, about 15 minutes. Spoon about ¼ cup of the filling down the center of each crepe. Roll up or fold. Spoon the remaining sauce over crepes to serve.

Note: For a variation, you can add 3 tablespoons chopped pimiento and ⅛ teaspoon garlic powder to the basic crepe batter.

Chicken Royale

A blend of cheese and herbs adds a distinctive touch to this variation of Chicken Divan. The recipe makes 6 (2-crepe) servings.

2 packages (10 ounces each) frozen broccoli spears
1 can (10½ ounces) condensed cream of mushroom soup
½ cup sherry
1 teaspoon Worcestershire sauce
½ teaspoon savory
¼ teaspoon pepper
3 chicken breast halves, cooked and sliced
4 slices American cheese cut in thirds
12 crepes

Cook the broccoli according to the package directions; drain. In a medium saucepan, combine the soup, sherry, Worcestershire sauce, savory and pepper. Cook over low heat until blended, stirring occasionally. Slice through the broccoli spears to form thin strips. Place equal amounts of broccoli and chicken in the crepes. Place a slice of cheese on top of the chicken. Roll up or fold. Arrange in a greased shallow baking dish or pan. Spoon the mushroom sauce over the crepes. Bake in a preheated 350°F oven 15 minutes.

Chicken Teriyaki Crepes

Marinated chicken is wrapped in crepes with a special sweet-sour sauce for an Americanized version of a Far East favorite. The recipe yields 4 (2-crepe) servings.

½ cup soy sauce
2 tablespoons sugar
1 teaspoon grated fresh ginger
1 clove garlic, minced
4 chicken breast halves, boned
8 crepes
Pineapple Sweet and Sour Sauce

Combine the soy sauce, sugar, ginger, garlic and chicken breasts in a shallow baking dish or heavy plastic bag. Add the chicken and refrigerate at least 2 hours, or overnight, turning the chicken in marinade occasionally. Broil the chicken, basting it with marinade, until done. Cut it into chunks. Spread about 1 tablespoon Pineapple Sweet and Sour Sauce on each crepe. Divide the chicken evenly between the crepes. Roll up or fold. Pour the remaining sauce over the crepes.

Pineapple Sweet and Sour Sauce

1 can (8 ounces) crushed pineapple
1 tablespoon brown sugar
1 tablespoon vinegar
2 teaspoons cornstarch

Place all the ingredients in a small saucepan. Cook and stir over medium-high heat until the mixture comes to a boil and is smooth and thickened.

Country Chicken

The black olives and tomatoes give this recipe a hearty flavor. Try these crepes for a brunch or patio supper. The recipe makes 8 servings of 2 crepes each or 2 or 3 small crepes each.

½ cup chopped onion
½ cup chopped green pepper
1 clove garlic, minced
3 tablespoons butter
2 tablespoons flour
½ cup dry white wine
4 tomatoes, peeled, chopped
1 teaspoon oregano, crushed
½ teaspoon salt
¼ teaspoon pepper
3 cups cubed, cooked chicken
1 cup pitted ripe olives, sliced
16 large or 24 small crepes

Saute' the onion, green pepper and garlic in butter until tender. Blend in the flour. Add the wine; cook and stir until smooth and thickened. Add the remaining ingredients, except the chicken and olives. Cover and simmer 20 minutes. Stir in the chicken and olives. Spoon about ¼ cup of the filling down the center of each large crepe; spoon 3 tablespoons down the center of each small crepe. Roll up or fold. Spoon the remaining sauce on top and serve.

Mandarin Chicken Crepes

Fruited sweet-sour sauce and crisp water chestnuts are the special features in this recipe. The recipe makes 8 (2-crepe) servings.

    ¾ cup chicken broth
    ¾ cup orange juice
    ¾ cup white wine
    ¼ cup lemon juice
    ¼ cup brown sugar
    3 tablespoons cornstarch
    1 can (11 ounces) mandarin oranges, drained
    4 cups cubed cooked chicken
    1 can (5 ounces) water chestnuts, drained and sliced
   16 crepes

In a saucepan, combine the chicken broth, orange juice, white wine, lemon juice, brown sugar and cornstarch. Cook and stir over medium heat until the mixture comes to a boil and is smooth and thickened. Add the mandarin oranges. In a small bowl, combine the chicken, water chestnuts and 1½ cups of the sauce. Divide the chicken mixture evenly among the crepes. Roll up or fold. Arrange them in a greased dish or pan. Spoon the sauce over crepes. Bake in a preheated 375°F oven 15 to 20 minutes.

126

Southern Chicken and Ham Crepes

Chicken, ham and peanuts are a favorite Southern combination. This recipe is a delicious example of that flavor trio. The recipe makes 6 (2-crepe) servings.

- ¼ cup butter
- ¼ cup flour
- 1¾ cups milk
- ¼ cup sherry
- ⅓ cup Parmesan cheese
- 1 teaspoon Dijon-style mustard
- 1 teaspoon salt
- ¼ teaspoon pepper
- 4 cups cubed, cooked chicken
- ½ cup peanut butter
- 12 thin slices ham
- 12 large crepes

Melt the butter in a saucepan. Add the flour and cook and stir until frothy. Add the milk and cook and stir over medium-high heat until smooth and thickened. Add the sherry, Parmesan cheese, mustard, salt and pepper. Simmer 2 to 3 minutes. Combine the chicken with 1 cup of the sauce. Spread 2 teaspoons peanut butter on each crepe, then top each crepe with 1 slice of ham. Spoon a generous ¼ cup of the chicken filling on each crepe. Roll up and arrange them in a greased shallow baking dish or pan. Pour the remaining sauce over the crepes. Bake in a preheated 400°F oven 8 to 10 minutes.

Crepes Caruso

Chicken livers simmer in an herbed tomato sauce before you wrap them in tender crepes. The recipe makes 4 servings.

> 2 tablespoons butter
> 1 small onion, chopped
> ½ pound chicken livers
> 1 can (8 ounces) tomato sauce
> ½ teaspoon basil
> ½ teaspoon garlic salt
> ¼ cup grated Parmesan cheese
> 4 large or 8 small crepes

Melt the butter in a skillet. Add the onion and cook over medium heat until tender, stirring often. Add the chicken livers and cook over medium-high heat just until done. Lift the livers from the skillet and chop coarsely. Return them to the skillet along with the tomato sauce, basil and garlic salt. Heat to boiling, then lower the heat and simmer 5 to 10 minutes. Sprinkle Parmesan cheese over the crepes, then spoon ¼ cup of filling down the center of each large crepe; spoon 2 tablespoons down the center of each small crepe. Roll up. If the crepes were not hot when filled, arrange them in a greased baking dish or pan and heat in a preheated 350°F oven about 15 minutes.

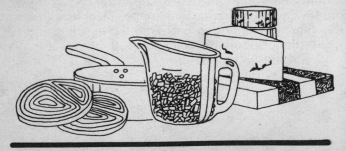

The Crepe Gallery

Melba Crepes Gateau—a dessert star! Peaches and whipped cream fill crepe layers, raspberries top it all.

Ham and Cheese Crepe Stack is an impressive, but very easy appetizer. Chill, then cut in wedges to serve.

Chicken Crepes Supreme—a reputation-making recipe to highlight any elegant brunch, dinner or supper.

Crab Crepes Francisco rival the best that any creperie can offer. Your guests will be impressed.

Apricot Crepes taste just as rich, golden and delicious as they look. Quarter-folded crepes are a change of pace.

Guacamole Crepes go south of the border. Smooth avocado mixes with spunky seasonings, lettuce and tomato.

Gulf Coast Crepes could become the standard in your crepe repertoire, and they couldn't be simpler to make.

Cottage Cheese Crepes take on almost any sauces or flavorings you wish—melon balls, strawberries, or spices.

Flaming Banana Butterscotch Crepes make a spectacular finish to any meal, or can be an occasion all by themselves.

Parmesan Crepe Crisps—a delectable way to use up less-than-perfect or left-over crepes.

Perfect Blintzes, an Old-World recipe brought up to date. Creamy filling is tucked inside the crepe pockets.

Crepes Champignon feature fresh mushrooms swimming in a savory sauce and wrapped in lacy-light crepes.

Chicken Liver Stroganoff Crepes

To delight the Epicurean, consider this sumptuous entree. The recipe makes 8 (2-crepe) servings.

    1 pound chicken livers
    ⅓ cup butter
    1 teaspoon salt
    ½ teaspoon pepper
    ½ pound mushrooms, sliced
    1 can (10¾ ounces) cream of mushroom soup
    1 cup dairy sour cream
   16 crepes

In large skillet, saute' the chicken livers in butter, salt and pepper until just done. Remove and chop. Add the mushrooms to the skillet; cover and cook until soft. Add the mushroom soup and chicken livers to the skillet. Stir in the sour cream and heat, but do not boil. Fill each crepe with ¼ cup of the mixture. Roll up or fold. Spoon the remaining sauce on top.

Sautéed Chicken Liver Crepes

For those who like chicken livers, these crepes are a gastronomical delight. You will have 16 filled crepes — enough for 8 generous or 16 smaller servings.

¼ pound bacon, chopped
¾ pound chicken livers
1 teaspoon seasoned salt
¼ teaspoon ground pepper
½ pound fresh mushrooms, sliced
2 tablespoons minced onion
¾ cup white wine
2 tablespoons butter
2 teaspoons tarragon
1 tablespoon flour
3 tablespoons wine or water
16 crepes

Fry the bacon until crisp in a large skillet. Reserve the drippings. Drain the bacon and set it aside in a small bowl. Saute' the chicken livers in the drippings. Season with the salt and pepper. Remove the livers and chop; place them in the bowl with the bacon. Add the mushrooms, onions, wine, butter and tarragon to same skillet. Cover and cook until the mushrooms are tender, about 10 to 15 minutes. Lift the mushrooms from the skillet and add them to the bowl with the livers and bacon. Toss together. Add the flour and the 3 tablespoons wine to the remaining liquid in the skillet. Cook over medium heat, stirring constantly until thickened and smooth. Stir in the chicken liver mixture until hot through. Spoon about 2 tablespoons of the mixture onto each crepe. Roll up or fold. To serve, pour the remaining sauce over the crepes. Serve immediately or arrange in a greased shallow baking dish or pan and heat in a preheated 350°F oven 10 minutes.

Golden Turkey Crab Stroganoff

Leftover turkey becomes entertaining fare with this recipe — it makes 6 savory servings.

- ½ cup chopped onions
- 2 tablespoons butter
- 2 cups cooked turkey, cubed
- 1 can (7½ ounces) crabmeat
- 1 can (10¾ ounces) condensed golden mushroom soup
- 1 cup dairy sour cream
- 1 teaspoon salt
- ½ teaspoon pepper
- 12 crepes

In a medium saucepan, saute' the onions in butter until tender. Add the remaining ingredients. Cover and cook over low heat about 10 to 15 minutes. Fill each crepe with ¼ cup of the mixture. Roll up or fold. Serve at once, spooning any remaining sauce over the top. Or, arrange the crepes in a greased baking dish. Spoon the remaining filling over top and heat in a preheated 350°F oven 10 to 15 minutes.

Sweet-Sour Turkey Crepes

So good you will want to buy a bigger-than-usual bird so you can enjoy this handsome disguise for leftover turkey. The recipe makes 6 servings.

1½ cups pineapple juice
½ cup firmly packed brown sugar
½ cup cider vinegar
2 tablespoons soy sauce
2 tablespoons cornstarch
¼ teaspoon ground ginger
¼ teaspoon garlic powder
2 cups diced cooked turkey
 Oil
2 carrots, thin-sliced
1 onion, thin-sliced
1 green pepper, thin-sliced
1 cup thin-sliced celery
12 large crepes

In a saucepan, combine the juice, brown sugar, vinegar, soy sauce, cornstarch and seasonings. Cook and stir over medium-high heat until the mixture comes to a boil and is smooth and thickened. Stir in the turkey and keep it warm. Heat the oil in a skillet. Add the vegetables and cook and stir over high heat about 3 minutes or until crisp and tender. Stir the vegetables into turkey-sauce mixture. Spoon about ½ cup of the mixture down the center of each crepe. Roll up or fold, spooning any remaining sauce over the crepes. Serve at once, or arrange the crepes in greased baking dish or pan and heat in a preheated 350°F oven about 15 minutes.

Turkey Cashew Crepes

Here is a crepe recipe that is rich, creamy and also crunchy with cashews. The recipe makes 8 (2-crepe) servings.

½ cup chopped onion
1½ cups chopped celery
3 tablespoons butter
1 can (10¾ ounces) condensed cream of mushroom soup
¾ cup light cream or evaporated milk
½ cup chicken broth or white wine
3 cups cooked cubed turkey
2 cups salted cashews
1½ cups grated Swiss cheese
16 crepes

Saute' the onion and celery in butter until tender. Stir in the mushroom soup, cream and chicken broth until smooth. Add the turkey and 1 cup of the cashews. Fill each crepe with about ¼ cup of the turkey filling and a generous 2 tablespoons of cheese. Roll the crepes and arrange them in a greased, shallow baking dish. Spoon remaining sauce over them. Sprinkle with the remaining cashews. Bake in a preheated 400°F oven 5 to 10 minutes or until bubbly and cheese is melted.

Main Dish Crepes with Ham, Pork and Sausage

Blanketed in tasty sauces and wrapped in delicate crepes, ham never had it so good. Leftover ham can make elegant encores when combined with asparagus, mushrooms, mellow Mornay Sauce or Piquant Cherry Sauce. Be sure to consider Apricot Brunch Crepes for your next brunch.

Creamy Asparagus Ham Crepes

A little ham goes a long way in these colorful crepes. The recipe makes 8 servings of 1 large crepe or 2 small crepes each.

- 1 package (10 ounces) frozen asparagus spears or 24 fresh asparagus spears
- 1 cup dairy sour cream
- ½ cup shredded Swiss, Monterey Jack, Brick or Cheddar cheese
- ¼ cup chopped pimiento
- 1 cup diced ham
- 8 large or 16 small crepes

Cook the frozen asparagus as the package directs; clean fresh asparagus and cook it just until tender. Combine the sour cream, cheese and pimiento, then stir in the ham. Spread about 2 tablespoons of the ham-cream mixture on each large crepe. Spread 1 tablespoon on each small crepe. Place 3 asparagus spears on each large crepe; place 1½ spears on each small crepe. Roll up or fold. Arrange the crepes in a greased baking dish or pan and bake in a preheated 350°F oven 15 to 20 minutes.

Creamy Caraway Ham Crepes

You will want to buy more ham than you really need for Sunday dinner, just so there will be enough left over for these delicious crepes. The recipe makes 6 servings of 1 large or 2 small crepes each.

1½ cups diced ham
1 cup dairy sour cream
1 tablespoon caraway seeds
1 tablespoon instant minced onion
1 tablespoon Worcestershire sauce
¼ teaspoon seasoned salt
6 large or 12 small crepes
¼ cup fine dry white or rye bread crumbs
2 tablespoons butter, melted

Combine the ham, sour cream, caraway seed, onion, Worcestershire sauce and salt. Spread about ¼ cup of the filling over each large crepe. Spread 2 tablespoons over each small crepe. Roll up or fold and arrange on a greased baking sheet. Toss the crumbs and melted butter together and sprinkle them over the crepes. Bake them in a preheated 400°F oven 5 to 10 minutes, or just until crumbs are browned.

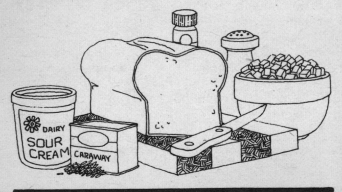

Creamy Ham Crepes with Cherry Nut Sauce

A tasty encore for leftover ham. The sauce couldn't be easier since you start with a can of cherry pie filling. The recipe makes 6 (2-crepe) servings.

    1 package (8 ounces) cream cheese
    2 tablespoons dairy sour cream
    1 tablespoon chopped chives
    3 cups julienne strips ham (¼ in. x 4 in.)
 12 crepes
    Cherry Nut Sauce

Beat the cream cheese, sour cream and chives together and spread a heaping tablespoon over each crepe. Top with several strips of ham. Roll up or fold and arrange on a greased baking sheet. Bake in a preheated 350°F oven 10 minutes. Spoon Cherry Nut Sauce over the crepes to serve.

Cherry Nut Sauce

    1 can (1 pound 5 ounces) cherry pie filling
    2 tablespoons lemon juice
    2 tablespoons water
    ½ teaspoon nutmeg
    ½ cup pecan halves

In a saucepan, combine the pie filling, lemon juice, water and nutmeg. Simmer 5 to 10 minutes, stirring occasionally. Stir in the pecans.

Dilled Ham Crepes

Unexpected company? With crepes on hand in the freezer or refrigerator, you can put together this recipe in mere minutes. The recipe makes 8 servings.

1 can (11 ounces) Cheddar cheese soup
1 medium green pepper, chopped
2 tablespoons milk
1 teaspoon lemon juice
½ teaspoon dried dill weed or seed
2 cups ground cooked ham
16 small or 8 large crepes

Combine the soup, green pepper, milk, lemon juice and dill. Add half the soup mixture to the ham and mix. Spread ¼ cup of the ham mixture over each large crepe; spread 2 tablespoons over each small crepe. Roll up and arrange in greased baking dish or pan. Spoon the remaining soup mixture over the crepes. Bake in a preheated 350°F oven 20 to 25 minutes or until bubbly.

Ham and Asparagus Crepes Mornay

These multipurpose crepes are delicious for brunch, supper, lunch, dinner, buffets—or any time. The recipe makes 6 servings of 2 large or 4 small crepes each.

> 1 pound fresh asparagus
> 2 tablespoons butter
> 2 tablespoons flour
> 1 cup milk or half and half
> 1 tablespoon instant minced onion
> ½ teaspoon salt
> ¼ teaspoon dry mustard
> ¼ cup grated Parmesan cheese
> 12 thin slices ham
> 12 thin slices Swiss cheese
> 3 tablespoons Dijon-style mustard
> 12 large or 24 small crepes

Clean the asparagus and cook it in boiling, salted water until tender. Meanwhile, melt the butter in a saucepan. Blend in the flour and cook and stir until frothy. Add the milk and seasonings and cook and stir over medium-high heat until smooth and thickened. Stir in the Parmesan cheese and remove the pan from the heat. Drain the asparagus and pat dry. Spread each large crepe with 1 teaspoon mustard; spread each small crepe with ½ teaspoon mustard. Arrange 1 ham slice, 1 cheese slice and 2 to 3 spears of asparagus on each large crepe; arrange ½ slice each of ham and cheese and 1 or 2 asparagus spears on each small crepe. Roll up or fold the crepes and arrange them in a greased baking dish or pan. Pour the sauce over them. Bake in a preheated 350°F oven 10 to 15 minutes.

Ham Crepes Bombay

Mildly flavored with curry, these sophisticated crepes receive additional flavor from the chutney. The recipe makes 4 to 8 servings.

- *1 can (1 pound 4 ounces) pineapple chunks*
- *1 tablespoon cornstarch*
- *1 teaspoon curry powder*
- *2 cups cubed cooked ham*
- *¼ cup chopped chutney*
- *1 tablespoon lemon or lime juice*
- *8 large crepes*
- *1 cup shredded Cheddar cheese*

Drain the pineapple, reserving the syrup. In a saucepan, blend the syrup, cornstarch and curry powder. Cook and stir over medium heat until the mixture comes to a boil and is smooth and thickened. Add the ham, chutney, pineapple and lime juice and heat through. Spoon about ⅓ cup of the filling down the center of each crepe. Roll up or fold. Arrange on a heat-proof platter, greased baking dish or pan. Spoon any remaining filling over the crepes. Sprinkle with cheese. Broil 5 to 6 inches from the heat about 3 minutes or until the cheese melts.

Ham Crepes Mornay

Mornay Sauce is cream sauce with several extras—
Swiss and Parmesan cheeses and distinct but subtle
seasonings. Parmesan Crepes would be a good choice
to harmonize with the filling. This recipe makes 8
crepes.

¼	cup butter
¼	cup flour
½	teaspoon dry mustard
¼	teaspoon salt
	Dash each black and cayenne pepper
2¼	cups milk
½	cup shredded Swiss cheese
¼	cup grated Parmesan cheese
2	cups cubed ham
½	pound fresh mushrooms, sliced
2	tablespoons butter
1	tablespoon chopped parsley
8	large crepes

Melt the ¼ cup butter in a saucepan. Add the flour and
seasonings; cook and stir until frothy. Add the milk and
cook and stir over medium-high heat until smooth and
thickened. Stir in the cheese until melted. Combine 1
cup of the sauce with the ham. In a small skillet, cook
the mushrooms in the 2 tablespoons butter until tender.
Stir the mushrooms into the ham mixture along with the
parsley. Spoon about ⅓ cup of the ham-mushroom mixture down the center of each crepe and roll up or fold.
Arrange the crepes in a greased baking dish or pan.
Spoon any remaining filling over them, then spoon the
rest of the Mornay sauce over the top. Bake the crepes
in a preheated 350°F oven 20 minutes.

Ham Mushroom Crepes

Ham for Sunday dinner can mean extra-special and extra-easy crepes for Monday or Tuesday supper. The recipe makes 8 servings.

2 cups cubed cooked ham (or turkey or roast beef)
1 can (10½ ounces) cream of mushroom soup
1 can (4 ounces) sliced mushrooms and liquid
1 tablespoon instant minced onion
1 tablespoon lemon juice
1 tablespoon chopped parsley
8 large or 16 small crepes

Combine the ham, soup, mushrooms, onion, lemon juice and parsley. Spoon about ¼ cup down the center of each large crepe; spoon 2 tablespoons down the center of each small crepe. Roll up or fold. Arrange the crepes in a greased baking dish or pan. Spoon any remaining ham mixture over the top. Bake in a preheated 350°F oven 20 minutes.

Ham Rolls with Cherry Sauce

The piquant Cherry Sauce makes this an exceptional main dish. The recipe makes 8 servings.

> 2 cups minced ham
> ½ cup fine dry bread crumbs
> 1 egg
> 1 teaspoon dry mustard
> ½ teaspoon salt
> 8 crepes
>   Cherry Sauce

Mix together the ham, dry bread crumbs, egg, dry mustard and salt. Divide the mixture into 8 sections; roll each into a log shape. Place one log on each crepe. Roll up or fold. Put the crepes in a greased shallow baking dish or pan. Spoon the sauce over the top. Bake in a preheated 350°F oven 20 to 25 minutes.

Cherry Sauce

> 1 can (21 ounces) cherry pie filling
> 1 teaspoon grated lemon peel
> 3 tablespoons lemon juice
> ⅛ teaspoon ground nutmeg

Combine all the ingredients, mixing thoroughly.

Spicy Peach Proscuitto Crepes

An unusual flavor combination but well worth tasting for brunch, lunch or supper. The recipe makes 6 servings.

    1 jar (18 ounces) spiced peaches
    2 tablespoons vinegar
    1 tablespoon brown sugar
    1 tablespoon cornstarch
    1 teaspoon minced onion
    ¼ pound proscuitto, chopped
    6 crepes

Drain the peaches, reserve ¾ cup of juice. Pit the peaches and chop. In a small saucepan, stir together the peach juice, brown sugar, cornstarch, vinegar and onion. Cook over medium heat, stirring constantly until thickened. Stir in the peaches. Place an equal amount of chopped proscuitto on each crepe. Spoon 2 tablespoons of the spiced peach mixture in each crepe's center. Roll.

Apple 'N Pork Crepes

The sweet and spice combination of sauerkraut and brown sugar gives these crepes a special flavor. The crepes are served with Saucy Apples. The recipe makes 6 servings of 2 crepes each.

    2 tablespoons chopped onion
    2 tablespoons brown sugar
    2 tablespoons butter
    1 cup sauerkraut, drained
    1 teaspoon cinnamon
    2 cups chopped, cooked pork
    12 crepes
        Saucy Apples

Saute' the onion and brown sugar in butter until the onion is soft. Add the sauerkraut, cinnamon and pork. Simmer 15 minutes. Fill each crepe with about ¼ cup of the filling. Roll the crepes and serve them with hot Saucy Apples.

Saucy Apples

    1 can (1 pound 5 ounces) apple pie filling
    2 tablespoons lemon juice
    1 teaspoon cinnamon

Heat the apple pie filling, lemon juice and cinnamon together and keep them hot until serving.

Oriental Pork Crepes

You may also use diced chicken or beef in place of pork.
Garnish with pineapple chunks for an East meets West
treat. The recipe makes 6 servings.

    2 tablespoons butter or oil
    1 pound diced lean boneless pork
    1 medium onion, chopped
    1 clove garlic, minced
    ¼ cup soy sauce
    1 medium green pepper, chopped
    1 can (5 ounces) water chestnuts, drained and sliced
    1 can (1 pound) Chinese vegetables, drained
   12 large crepes

Melt the butter or heat the oil in a large skillet. Add the
pork, onion and garlic and brown lightly. Stir in the soy
sauce; cover and simmer about 10 minutes or until
tender. Add the vegetables. Spoon about ⅓ cup of the
filling down the center of each crepe. Fold or roll and
arrange in a greased baking dish or pan. Heat in a preheated 350°F oven about 20 minutes.

Apricot Brunch Crepes

Search no more for a recipe to star at weekend brunches — this is the one. The recipe makes 6 servings.

24 link sausages
1 can (17 ounces) apricot halves
3 tablespoons wine vinegar
¼ cup chopped green pepper or celery
2 tablespoons minced onion
6 large or 12 small crepes

Brown the sausages in a skillet. Drain off the fat. Drain the apricots, reserving ½ cup syrup. Add the syrup, vinegar, green pepper (or celery) and onions to the sausages, cover and simmer about 5 minutes or until the sausage is done. Add the apricots and heat thoroughly. Arrange 2 sausage links in the center of each large crepe; put one sausage in the center of each small crepe. Roll up or fold. Spoon the apricot mixture over the crepes to serve.

Sausage Pizza Crepes

These pizza crepes are a Franco-Italian-American alliance that can be served as hearty appetizers, as a brunch entree or for supper. The recipe makes 8 main dish servings.

- 1 can (8 ounces) tomato sauce
- ¼ teaspoon oregano
- ¼ teaspoon thyme
- ¼ teaspoon salt
- ⅛ teaspoon pepper
  Dash garlic powder
- 1 cup shredded Mozzarella cheese
- ¼ pound bulk sausage, cooked and drained
- 8 crepes

Combine the tomato sauce and spices. Spread about 2 tablespoons of sauce on each crepe. Sprinkle each with 2 tablespoons of cheese. Divide the sausage evenly on top. Fold in half, then fold into a triangle. Place the crepes on a greased baking sheet. Cover with foil. Bake in a preheated 400°F oven 5 minutes or until the cheese is melted.

Main Dish Crepes with Seafood

Some of the best loved main dish crepes are sea-food crepes — Crepes St. Jacques with shrimp, scallops and crab in a rich sauce and Crab Crepes Alaska with a whiff of sherry in the sauce. You can make a small amount of seafood stretch to serve company for dinner with these recipes. Salmon Quiche Crepes and Oyster Stuffed Crepes are some of the seafood surprises in this section.

Asparagus Filet Crepes

Worthy of a most important occasion! This recipe makes 4 servings of 2 large crepes each.

- 1 pound frozen fish fillets, thawed
- 2 cans (10¾ ounces each) condensed cream of mushroom soup
- ¼ cup white wine
- 1 can (4 ounces) sliced mushrooms, drained
- ¼ cup grated Parmesan cheese
- 1 tablespoon lemon juice
- 1 teaspoon Worcestershire sauce
- 1 teaspoon salt
- ½ teaspoon pepper
- 8 crepes
- 2 cans (14½ ounces each) asparagus spears, drained
  Parmesan cheese
- ½ cup sliced toasted almonds

Poach the fish fillets in a small amount of simmering salted water until the fish flakes easily when a fork is inserted. Drain the fish and cut it into chunks. Set aside. In a large saucepan, combine the soup, wine, mushrooms, Parmesan cheese, lemon juice, Worcestershire sauce, salt and pepper; simmer about 10 minutes. Gently stir together 1 cup of the sauce and the fish chunks. Divide the asparagus spears among crepes, then spoon about ¼ cup of the fish filling down the center of each crepe. Roll up or fold. Arrange the crepes in a greased, shallow baking dish or pan. Spoon the remaining sauce over them. Sprinkle with additional Parmesan cheese and almonds. Broil until lightly browned.

Crab and Cheddar Crepes

This savory crepe recipe can be prepared in advance, covered and stored in the refrigerator until you are ready to heat it up. Add an extra 5 or 10 minutes of baking time if crepes have been refrigerated. The recipe makes 6 servings of one large or 2 small crepes each.

- 1 package (6 ounces) frozen crab meat, thawed
- 2 hard-cooked eggs, chopped
- ½ cup chopped celery
- ½ cup shredded Cheddar cheese
- ⅓ cup mayonnaise or salad dressing
- ¼ cup chopped sweet pickle
- ½ teaspoon salt
- ¼ teaspoon dry mustard
  Dash pepper
- 6 large or 12 small crepes

Drain and flake the crabmeat. Combine the crab with the eggs, celery, cheese, mayonnaise, pickle and seasonings. Spoon about ⅓ cup onto each large crepe; spoon 3 tablespoons onto each small crepe. Fold the crepes in quarter-folds or roll them up. Arrange the crepes on a greased cookie sheet or baking pan and bake in a preheated 350°F oven 15 to 20 minutes.

Crab Crepes Alaska

Just a whiff of sherry adds elegance to the sauce of these crepes. If you want to match the crepes served in a creperie, this is the recipe to try. Use Parmesan Crepes with this filling. The recipe makes 8 crepes for 4 generous portions or 8 single crepe servings.

½   small onion, chopped
¼   pound fresh mushrooms, sliced
¼   cup butter
2   tablespoons flour
¾   cup milk
1½ tablespoons sherry
½   teaspoon salt
⅛   teaspoon pepper
¼   teaspoon Worcestershire sauce
    Dash hot pepper sauce
1   can (7½ ounces) crab or 1 package (6 ounces) frozen crab, thawed
8   large crepes
¼   cup sliced almonds
1   tablespoon chopped parsley

In a saucepan or small skillet, cook the onion and mushrooms in butter until tender. Blend in the flour and cook until frothy. Add the milk and sherry and cook and stir until smooth and thickened. Stir in the seasonings. Drain and slice the crab and stir it into the sauce. Spread about 2 tablespoons of the filling over each crepe and roll up or fold. Arrange the crepes in a greased baking dish or pan. Spoon any remaining filling over them. Sprinkle with almonds and parsley. Bake in preheated 350°F oven 15 minutes.

Crab Crepes Francisco

Serve these simple crepes hot or cold. They are a nice addition to a brunch or buffet menu. The recipe makes 6 servings.

1 package (6 ounces) frozen crab, thawed
¼ cup chopped green onion or green pepper
¼ cup chopped celery
¼ cup dairy sour cream
¼ cup mayonnaise
1 teaspoon lemon or lime juice
¼ teaspoon seasoned salt
¼ teaspoon dry mustard
¼ teaspoon tarragon (optional)
6 crepes

Drain the crab meat and slice or flake. Mix the crab, onion, celery, sour cream, mayonnaise, juice and seasonings. Divide the crab mixture among the crepes and roll up or fold. Serve cold or arrange the crepes on a greased baking sheet and bake in a preheated 350°F oven 10 to 15 minutes.

Creamy Tuna Crepes Oriental

Instead of the usual clear sweet-sour sauce, this crepe filling is rich and thick. The recipe makes 4 generous servings or 8 single-crepe portions.

  1 can (9 ounces) tuna, drained and flaked
  1 can (10¾ ounces) condensed cream of mushroom soup, undiluted
  1 can (1 pound) Chinese vegetables, drained
  1 can (5 ounces) water chestnuts, drained and sliced
  ½ medium green pepper, chopped
  3 tablespoons lemon juice
  1 can (11 ounces) mandarin orange sections, drained (optional)
  8 large or 16 small crepes
  1 cup Chow Mein noodles

Combine the tuna, soup, vegetables, sliced water chestnuts, chopped pepper, lemon juice and oranges. Spoon about ¼ cup of the filling in the center of each large crepe; spoon 2 tablespoons in the center of each small crepe. Fold opposite sides to meet in the center, then fold the ends to meet in the center, as for blintzes (see Folding Crepes). Arrange in a greased baking dish or pan; pour any remaining tuna mixture over the crepes. Sprinkle with the noodles. Bake in a preheated 350°F oven 15 minutes.

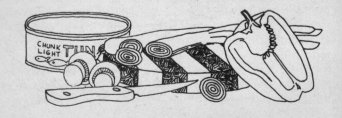

Crepes St. Jacques

These crepes have a rich cream filling with shrimp, scallops and crab. They are guaranteed to win you an ovation. The recipe makes 16 large crepes, enough for 8 dinner servings. If you use a frozen seafood, save any liquid from the package to use as a part of the liquid in making the sauce.

¼ cup butter
¼ cup flour
2 tablespoons instant minced onion
½ teaspoon dry mustard
¼ teaspoon salt
¼ teaspoon pepper
2 cups half and half (or seafood liquid plus half and half)
2 tablespoons sherry
4 to 6 ounces cooked scallops, halved
6 ounces cooked cleaned shrimp
6 ounces cooked crab
½ pound fresh mushrooms, sliced
2 tablespoons butter
16 large crepes

Melt the ¼ cup butter in a medium saucepan. Add the flour, onion and seasonings; cook and stir over medium-high heat until frothy. Add the half and half; cook and stir until the mixture is smooth and thickened. Stir in the sherry and seafood. In a small skillet, cook the mushrooms in butter until just tender. Stir the mushrooms into the seafood mixture. Spoon about ¼ cup of the seafood mixture into center of each crepe and roll up or fold. Arrange the crepes in a greased baking dish or pan. Spoon any remaining seafood mixture over them. Bake in a preheated 350°F oven about 15 to 20 minutes.

Curried Tuna Crepes

You mix together peanuts, raisins and coconut to serve along with these mildly curried crepes. The recipe makes 6 (2-crepe) servings.

2 tablespoons butter
1 apple, chopped
½ cup chopped onion
1 to 2 teaspoons curry powder
2 cans (6½-7 ounces each) tuna
1 can (10¾ ounces) condensed cream of celery soup
½ cup water
1 teaspoon salt
½ teaspoon pepper
½ teaspoon grated lemon peel (optional)
12 large crepes
⅓ cup chopped peanuts
⅓ cup chopped raisins
⅓ cup flaked coconut

Melt the butter in a medium skillet. Add the apple, onion and curry powder and cook until tender. Stir in the tuna, soup, water, salt, pepper and lemon peel. Simmer 15 minutes. Spoon about ¼ cup of the filling down the center of each crepe. Roll up or fold. Combine the peanuts, raisins and coconut and serve alongside as a condiment.

Fish Creole Crepes

Here is a delightful adaptation of a savory New Orleans recipe. The recipe will make 6 servings.

2 tablespoons butter
¼ cup chopped onion
2 tablespoons flour
2 cans (1 pound each) stewed tomatoes
½ teaspoon thyme
1 clove garlic, minced
1 pound frozen fish fillets, thawed
12 crepes

Melt the butter in a large saucepan. Sauté the onions until soft. Add the flour; stir and cook for 2 or 3 minutes. Add the tomatoes, thyme and garlic. Cook about 15 minutes. Poach the fish fillets in simmering, salted water until tender. Drain and break them into bite-sized pieces. Add the fish to the tomato sauce. Fill the crepes with about ¼ cup of the fish creole. Roll up. Pour any remaining sauce over the crepes to serve.

Gulf Coast Crepes

Shrimp can always be counted on to win rave reviews. The curry makes it a special treat. The recipe makes 6 to 8 servings.

¼ cup chopped onion
2 teaspoons curry powder
2 tablespoons butter
1 can (10¾ ounces) cream of shrimp soup
2 cups dairy sour cream
2 cups cooked shrimp
16 crepes

Saute' the onion and curry powder in the butter. Add the soup; stir and cook over medium heat. Stir in the sour cream and shrimp. Simmer about 5 minutes. Spoon about ¼ cup of the filling on each crepe. Roll up or fold and serve at once. Or, arrange the crepes in a greased baking dish or pan and heat in a preheated 350°F oven 10 minutes.

Island Fish Crepes

Although the combination of foods sounds strange, the flavor combinations are unbelievably delicious. The recipe makes 6 servings of 2 crepes each.

  2 pounds frozen fish fillets, thawed
  2 cups milk
  ⅔ cup rum or white wine
  1 teaspoon salt
  ¼ teaspoon pepper
  ¼ cup butter
  ¼ cup flour
  2 tablespoons minced onion
  ⅛ teaspoon nutmeg
  2 ounces bleu cheese
  3 bananas, peeled and quartered
 12 crepes

Poach the fish in the milk, rum, salt and pepper until the fish is done and flakes easily when tested with a fork. Remove the fish; cool and cut into chunks. Reserve 3 cups of the poaching liquid. Melt the butter, add the flour and cook until frothy. Add the poaching liquid, onion and nutmeg. Cook over medium heat until thickened and smooth. Remove half of the sauce; add the fish to it. Add the bleu cheese to the other half of the sauce. Place about 2 tablespoons fish and one quarter banana on each crepe. Roll up and arrange them in a greased, shallow baking dish or pan. Spoon the bleu cheese sauce on top. Bake in a preheated 400°F oven 10 minutes.

Oriental Crepes Supreme

Peanuts add an unexpected taste and delightful crunch, as well as helping ½ pound of shrimp stretch to fill 12 crepes. The recipe makes 6 (2-crepe) servings or 12 single crepe servings. Try Cornmeal or Whole Wheat Crepes with this filling.

    8   ounces cooked shrimp, chopped
    1   cup chopped peanuts
    ½   cup chopped celery
    ½   cup sliced water chestnuts
    2   tablespoons sliced green onion
    1½ tablespoons soy sauce
    1   tablespoon sherry
    ½   teaspoon salt
    ¼   teaspoon ground ginger
    12 large crepes
    1   cup dairy sour cream
    1   teaspoon grated onion
    1   tablespoon flour
    1   teaspoon dry mustard
    ½   cup milk
    1   egg yolk

In a bowl, combine the shrimp, peanuts, celery, water chestnuts, onion, soy sauce, sherry, salt and ginger. Toss to mix. Spoon about ¼ cup of the mixture down the center of each crepe and roll up or fold. Arrange the crepes in a greased baking dish or on a greased baking sheet and bake in a preheated 350°F oven 20 minutes. Meanwhile, combine the sour cream, onion, flour and mustard in a saucepan. Blend in the milk. Cook and stir over medium heat until the mixture comes to a boil. Remove the pan from the heat. Beat the egg yolk and stir a small amount of the hot mixture into it. Blend the egg yolk mixture with the rest of the sauce in the pan. Spoon the mustard sauce over hot crepes to serve.

Oyster Stuffed Crepes

Not a simple recipe, these extraordinarily delicious crepes combine oysters, shallots, wine and spinach. The recipe makes 6 (2-crepe) servings.

- 2 pints oysters
- 2 tablespoons finely-chopped shallots
- ½ cup dry white wine
- 1 teaspoon salt
- ¼ teaspoon pepper
- ⅛ teaspoon nutmeg
- ¼ teaspoon cayenne pepper
- 3 egg yolks, beaten
- 1 cup whipping cream or liquid non-dairy creamer
- 2 packages (10 ounces each) frozen chopped spinach, cooked, drained
- 1 tablespoon lemon juice
- 12 crepes
- ¼ pound bacon, chopped, cooked crisp

Drain the oyster liquid into a saucepan. Add the shallots, wine, salt, pepper, nutmeg, cayenne pepper. Cook until the liquid is reduced almost by half. Beat the egg yolks and cream together. Beat in a little hot liquid with the eggs, return the eggs to the saucepan. Add the oysters. Cook and stir until thickened but do not boil. Mix the spinach and lemon juice. Spoon about 2 tablespoons spinach on each crepe and roll up. Arrange them in a greased baking dish or pan. Spoon the oyster sauce over them. Bake in a preheated 350°F oven 5 minutes. Sprinkle cooked crisp bacon over the crepes to serve.

Salmon Crepes with Mousseline Sauce

The term Mousseline means that a sauce is enriched with whipping cream or heavy cream. The sauce makes these crepes as mellow and rich as possible. The recipe makes 8 servings.

 2 cans (1 pound each) salmon, drained
 1 pint (2 cups) dairy sour cream
 2 tablespoons grated onion
 ¼ cup lemon juice
 ½ teaspoon salt
 ¼ teaspoon pepper
 1 teaspoon dried dill weed
16 crepes
   Mousseline Sauce

In a saucepan, combine the salmon, dairy sour cream, onion, lemon juice, salt and pepper and dill weed. Sim-

mer about 5 minutes. Spoon about ¼ cup of the filling down the center of each crepe. Roll up or fold and arrange on a serving dish or plate. Spoon the Mousseline Sauce on top to serve.

Mousseline Sauce

1 cup heavy cream
2 egg yolks
½ cup butter
⅓ cup lemon juice
½ teaspoon salt
Dash pepper

Beat the cream with the egg yolks. Melt the butter in a saucepan. Stir in the egg and cream mixture, lemon juice, salt and pepper. Cook and stir over low heat until it is slightly thickened.

Salmon Quiche Crepes

Quiche sounds difficult, but really it is just a simple custard pie that is not sweet. Quiche crepes combine two favorite French dishes. You use small crepes (or trimmed large ones) instead of a pastry shell. This recipe makes 12 individual quiches.

    3 eggs
    1 cup milk
    1 tablespoon instant minced onion
    1 tablespoon parsley flakes
    1 teaspoon seasoned salt
    ¼ teaspoon pepper
    1 teaspoon grated lemon peel
    1 tablespoon lemon juice
    1 can (1 pound) salmon, drained and flaked
   12 small crepes
    ¼ cup grated Parmesan cheese

Beat the eggs slightly. Stir in the milk and seasonings, lemon peel, lemon juice, and then the salmon. Generously grease 12 muffin cups and fit the crepes in them. (The crepes must not have any holes in them.) Divide the egg-salmon mixture among the cups. Sprinkle the crepes with Parmesan cheese. Bake in a preheated 350°F oven 25 to 30 minutes, or until a knife inserted off-center comes out clean.

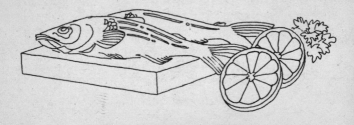

Sole Crepes Marguery

The ultimate in subtle, sophisticated flavors, Marguery Sauce is made the quick way from shrimp soup. The recipe makes 6 (2-crepe) servings.

   2 pounds fresh or frozen sole fillets
   1 cup vermouth or chicken broth
   1 tablespoon lemon juice
   1 tablespoon grated onion
   1 teaspoon salt
   ½ teaspoon pepper
   2 cans (10¾ ounces each) condensed cream of
     shrimp soup
   1 cup cooked small shrimp
   2 tablespoons chopped parsley
  12 crepes
     Lemon wedges
     Parsley

Poach the sole in the vermouth, lemon juice, onion, salt and pepper until tender. Remove the fish and section into 12 portions. Reserve 1 cup of poaching liquid. In a medium saucepan, blend the cream of shrimp soup, reserved poaching liquid, and heat through. When ready to serve add the shrimp and parsley. Set aside 1 cup of the shrimp sauce for topping. Add the sole to remaining sauce. Spoon about ¼ cup of the filling down the center of each crepe. Roll up or fold. To serve, spoon the reserved shrimp sauce on top. Garnish with lemon wedges and parsley.

Curried Crab and Pear Crepes

Crunchy with vegetables and mildly spiced, these crepes make a memorable choice for a luncheon or special brunch. The recipe makes 6 servings of 2 large or 3 small crepes each.

  ½ cup mayonnaise
  1 teaspoon curry powder
  1 teaspoon salt
  1 cup canned or fresh bean sprouts, well drained
  ½ cup chopped green pepper
  ½ cup sliced water chestnuts
  ½ cup sliced green onion
  1 can (1 pound) pear halves, drained, chopped
  1 can (7½ ounces) crabmeat, drained
  12 large or 18 small crepes
  1 can (6 ounces) frozen avocado dip, thawed
    Tomato wedges
    Lemon slices

In a large bowl, stir together the mayonnaise, curry and salt. Fold in the bean sprouts, green pepper, water chestnuts, and green onion. Add the chopped pears and flaked crabmeat. Chill at least 2 hours. Spoon about ¼ cup of the filling down the center of each large crepe; spoon 3 tablespoons down the center of each small crepe. Roll up or fold. Spoon the avocado dip over the crepes to serve. Garnish with tomato wedges and lemon slices.

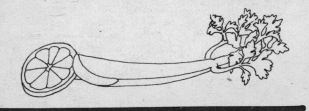

Sherried Crab and Cheese Crepes

This recipe makes one package of crab go a very long, very delicious way. This recipe could be featured at a shower or any other celebration. It makes 8 large servings, 16 small ones.

- 1 package (6 ounces) frozen crab meat, thawed
- 1 cup liquid (crab liquid plus milk)
- 2 tablespoons butter
- 2 tablespoons flour
- ¼ cup sherry
- 1 cup shredded Cheddar cheese
- 2 hard-cooked eggs, chopped
- 8 large or 16 small crepes

Drain the crab, reserving the liquid. Add milk to the liquid to make 1 cup. Melt the butter in a saucepan. Add the flour and cook and stir until frothy. Add the liquid and cook and stir over medium-high heat until mixture comes to a boil and is smooth and thickened. Remove it from the heat. Stir in the sherry, ½ cup of the cheese, the eggs and crab. Spread about 2 tablespoons over each small crepe. Arrange in a greased baking dish or pan. Sprinkle with the remaining ½ cup cheese. Bake in a preheated 350°F oven 20 to 25 minutes.

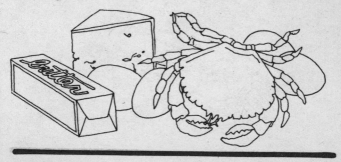

Shrimp Crepes Goldenrod

This is a beautiful way to serve shrimp without spending a lot. The recipe yields 6 servings.

    6   eggs, hard-cooked
    ¼ cup butter
    ¼ cup flour
    2   cups milk
    1   cup cooked shrimp
    2   tablespoons chopped onion
    1   teaspoon Worcestershire sauce
    ½ teaspoon salt
    ¼ teaspoon pepper
    12   crepes

Separate the yolks and whites of hard-cooked eggs. Slice the egg whites and set them aside. Force the egg yolks through a sieve. Melt the butter, add the flour and blend. Cook and stir until frothy. Add the milk, cook and stir over medium-high heat until the mixture comes to a boil and is smooth and thickened. Stir in the shrimp, egg whites, onion, Worcestershire sauce, salt and pepper. Fill the crepes with about ¼ cup of the mixture. Roll up. Sprinkle the egg yolk on top to serve.

Sweet and Sour Shrimp Crepes

Canned sauce helps you serve an elegant meal and still have energy to enjoy it with your guests. The recipe makes 6 (2-crepe) servings.

2 cans (11 ounces each) sweet and sour sauce
2 cups cooked shrimp
1 cup cherry tomatoes, sliced
1 cup green pepper slices
½ cup green onion, sliced
1 tablespoon soy sauce
12 crepes

Combine all the ingredients in a medium saucepan. Heat over medium heat about 15 minutes. Fill each crepe with about ¼ cup filling. Roll up or fold. Spoon the remaining sauce over the crepes to serve.

Newburg Crepes

Next time you have a covered dish to carry to a pot luck or church supper, give this recipe a try. Cover the hot baked crepes in a dish with foil, then wrap in several layers of newspaper to hold in the heat while transporting it. Serve right away—it is unwise to let warm food stand. The recipe makes 4 to 6 servings.

> 1 can (7½ or 9 ounces) tuna, drained and flaked
> 1 cup dairy sour cream
> ½ cup shredded Monterey Jack cheese
> ½ cup diced celery and/or green pepper
> ½ cup chopped pitted ripe olives
> ¼ cup chopped green onion or 1 tablespoon instant
>   minced onion
> 1 tablespoon lemon juice
> ½ teaspoon celery salt
> 8 large or 12 small crepes

Mix together the tuna, sour cream, cheese, celery, olives, onion, lemon juice and celery salt. Spoon about ¼ cup of the filling across the center of each large crepe; spoon about 3 tablespoons of filling into each small crepe. Fold or roll. Arrange the crepes in a greased baking dish or pan and bake in a preheated 350°F oven 20 minutes.

Crepes with Cheese, Eggs and Vegetables

Four versions of the popular Blintz lead off a parade of superb crepes. There is an irresistible Cinnamon Danish Crepe, as well as such brunch favorites as Eggs Benedict and Souffle' in Crepe Cups. Savory sauces and smooth cheese fillings complement an assortment of vegetables. You will even find a crunchy Waldorf Salad Crepe to serve as a salad or side dish.

Perfect Blintzes

You can easily double this tasty recipe to feed a crowd for lunch, brunch or dessert. The recipe makes 3 to 4 servings.

   1 cup small curd cottage cheese
   1 egg
   ¼ cup seedless raisins
   2 tablespoons sugar
   1 teaspoon cinnamon
   6 to 8 large crepes
   2 to 3 tablespoons butter
   ½ cup dairy sour cream

Mix together the cottage cheese, egg, raisins, sugar and cinnamon. Spoon about 1½ tablespoons of the cheese mixture in center of each crepe. Fold as for blintzes (see Folding Crepes). Melt the butter in a large skillet, then add the blintzes, seam side down. Brown lightly, then turn and brown the top. Top each blintz with a spoonful of sour cream.

Lemon Blintzes

You add a slight twist of lemon to the popular blintz and make a mellow lemon sauce for a brunch treat or dessert. The recipe makes 6 servings.

  2 cups cottage cheese
  1 egg, well beaten
  2 tablespoons sour cream
  1 tablespoon sugar
  1 tablespoon grated lemon peel
  ½ teaspoon salt
     Lemon Sauce
 12 crepes

In a mixing bowl, combine all the ingredients except the crepes and lemon sauce. Beat until thoroughly blended. Fill the browned side of each crepe with about 3 tablespoons filling. Fold the opposite sides together, then fold the ends to form a pocket (see Folding Crepes). Fry the blintzes in a hot, buttered skillet, turning once. Serve with Lemon Sauce.

Lemon Sauce

  1 cup water
  1 tablespoon butter
  ½ cup sugar
  3 tablespoons lemon juice
  1 tablespoon cornstarch
  1 teaspoon vanilla extract
  1 teaspoon grated lemon peel

Combine all the ingredients in a small saucepan. Cook and stir over medium heat until the mixture comes to a boil and is smooth and thickened.

Orange Blintzes

Fresh orange flavor in the filling and the Orange Sauce gives extra sparkle to these plump blintzes. Orange Crepes are perfect with the filling and sauce. The recipe makes 8 (2-blintz) servings.

 2 cups cream-style cottage cheese
 1 egg
 2 tablespoons sugar
 ¼ cup fine dry bread, cookie or cornflake crumbs
 1 teaspoon grated orange peel
16 large crepes
 2 tablespoons butter
   Orange Sauce
   Sour cream

In a small bowl, combine the cottage cheese, egg, sugar, crumbs and orange peel; beat until smooth. Place 3 tablespoons in center of each crepe. Fold one side over, then the other. Fold the remaining ends in. (See Folding Crepes.) Heat the butter in a large skillet and add blint-

zes, seam side down. Brown them slowly, then turn and brown other side. Prepare the sauce while the blintzes brown. Spoon warm Orange Sauce over the blintzes to serve. Top with sour cream.

Orange Sauce

    2 tablespoons cornstarch
    1 cup sugar
    ¼ teaspoon salt
    2 cups orange juice
    2 cups orange sections

Combine the cornstarch, sugar and salt in a saucepan. Stir in the orange juice. Cook and stir over medium-high heat until the mixture comes to a boil and is smooth and thickened. Simmer 1 minute. Remove from the heat, then stir in the orange sections.

Raspberry Blintzes

The rich cream cheese filling in the crepe "pockets" is a perfect complement to the tart-sweet Raspberry Sauce. Check back to Folding Crepes to see how to fold blintzes. Try making Orange Crepes for this recipe. The recipe makes 6 (2-crepe) servings.

    1 package (8 ounces) cream cheese, softened
    ¼ cup confectioners' sugar
    1 tablespoon lemon juice
    12 crepes
    2 to 4 tablespoons butter

Beat the cream cheese, sugar and lemon juice until smooth. Spoon about 1 tablespoonful in center of each crepe. Fold as for blintzes. Brown the blintzes seam side down in the butter in a skillet until golden. Turn and brown the other side. Prepare the sauce while the blintzes brown. Spoon the Raspberry Sauce over the hot blintzes to serve.

Raspberry Sauce

    1 package (10 ounces) frozen raspberries, thawed
    2 tablespoons kirsch
    1 tablespoon cornstarch

Drain the raspberries, reserving the syrup. In a saucepan, blend the syrup, kirsch and cornstarch; cook and stir until smooth and thickened. Stir in the raspberries and heat through.

California Curry Crepes

These fruited crepes go nicely as a side dish or on a party buffet. The recipe makes 8 large or 16 small crepes.

- 1 can (1 pound 13 ounces) cling peach slices
- 1½ tablespoons cornstarch
- 3 tablespoons sugar
- 1 teaspoon curry powder
- ½ teaspoon grated lemon peel
- 1 tablespoon lemon juice
- 1 tablespoon butter
- ½ cup chopped dates
- 8 large or 16 small crepes
- ½ cup chopped toasted almonds

Drain the peach slices, reserving the syrup. Measure the syrup and add water to make 1½ cups. In a saucepan, blend the cornstarch, sugar and curry powder. Stir in the syrup. Cook and stir over medium-high heat until the mixture comes to a boil and is smooth and thickened. Stir in the lemon peel, lemon juice and butter. Dice the peaches and add them to the sauce mixture along with the dates. Heat through. Roll the crepes up tightly or quarter-fold them and arrange in a chafing dish or on a serving platter. Spoon hot sauce over them and sprinkle with almonds to serve.

Lasagne Crepes

These delicately seasoned crepes can be assembled ahead of time and popped into the oven when you are ready to serve your guests. The recipe makes 6 (2-crepe) servings.

    1 tablespoon butter
    1 tablespoon flour
    1 cup milk
    1 teaspoon salt
    ⅛ teaspoon white pepper
    ⅛ teaspoon ground nutmeg
    ¾ cup grated Parmesan cheese
    ¼ pound Ricotta cheese
    1 egg
    ¼ cup shredded Mozzarella cheese
    ½ cup diced cooked ham
    1 can (16 ounces) spaghetti sauce
   12 crepes

Melt the butter in a saucepan; blend in flour and cook until frothy. Add milk, salt, pepper and nutmeg. Cook and stir over medium-high heat until mixture comes to a boil and is smooth and thickened. Blend in ½ cup of the Parmesan cheese. Remove from heat. In small bowl, combine Ricotta cheese and egg. Stir in Mozzarella cheese and ham; stir into cooled mixture. Spread about ¼ cup mixture on each crepe. Roll up or fold. Spoon ½ of the spaghetti sauce over bottom of greased shallow baking dish. Arrange filled crepes on sauce. Spoon remaining spaghetti sauce over and sprinkle with remaining Parmesan cheese. Refrigerate or immediately bake them in preheated 350°F oven 20 to 25 minutes.

Chili con Queso Crepes

If you enjoy spicy-hot foods, you can add ½ teaspoon chili powder to Cornmeal Crepe batter for this Mexican-type dish. The recipe makes 8 (2-crepe) servings.

1 can (1 pound) chili
2 cups shredded Cheddar cheese
1 cup chopped onion
1 can (8 ounces) taco sauce
16 large crepes

Fill each crepe with about 2 tablespoons each chili and cheese and 1 tablespoon each of the onion and taco sauce. Roll up or fold. Arrange the crepes on a greased baking sheet. Cover them lightly with foil. Bake in a preheated 400°F oven 8 to 10 minutes.
Note: For a variation you might use 1 can refried beans instead of chili.

Cinnamon Danish Crepes

A brunch spectacular! The recipe makes 6 to 8 servings.

       1 pound cottage cheese
       1 cup raisins
       2 tablespoons brown sugar
       1 teaspoon vanilla
       1 teaspoon cinnamon
      16 crepes
      ¼ cup sugar
      ¼ cup butter, melted
       1 tablespoon cinnamon

Stir together the cottage cheese, raisins, brown sugar, vanilla and 1 teaspoon cinnamon. Fill the crepes with 2 tablespoons of the mixture. Roll up. Place the crepes in a greased shallow baking dish or pan. Combine the sugar, butter and 1 tablespoon cinnamon. Drizzle over the crepes. Bake in a preheated 400°F oven 5 to 8 minutes.

Crepes Champignon

Swiss Mushroom Crepes taste just like those in the fanciest creperies. Toss a spinach salad and serve some French onion soup for a special dinner. The recipe makes 6 servings.

    1½ tablespoons butter
    1½ tablespoons flour
    ½   teaspoon salt
    ½   teaspoon dry mustard
    1   cup milk
    1   cup shredded Swiss cheese, divided
    1   tablespoon butter
    1   pound fresh mushrooms, sliced
    1   tablespoon lemon juice
    6   large or 12 small crepes

Melt the butter in a medium saucepan. Stir in the flour, salt and mustard; cook and stir over medium-high heat until frothy. Add the milk; cook and stir until the mixture comes to a boil and is smooth and thickened. Stir in half the cheese. In a skillet, melt 1 tablespoon butter. Add the mushrooms and cook and stir until tender. Stir in the lemon juice. Combine the mushroom mixture with the cheese sauce. Spoon about 2 tablespoons in center of each crepe; spoon 1 tablespoon of the mixture in the center of each small crepe. Roll up, fold in half or in quarters and arrange in greased baking dish or pan. Spoon remaining sauce over and sprinkle with the remaining cheese. Heat in a broiler 2 to 3 minutes, or until cheese melts, or heat in a preheated 350°F oven 20 minutes.

Denver Crepes with Cheese

Flavorful and filling, these crepes can star at a brunch or casual luncheon. Teens love them too, especially in Whole Wheat or Cornmeal Crepes. The recipe makes 8 large crepes. You could easily double the recipe for a crowd.

    4 hard-cooked eggs, chopped
    1 cup diced ham
    ½ cup shredded Swiss, Monterey Jack or Cheddar
       cheese
    ¼ cup chopped green pepper
    ¼ cup chopped dill pickle
    ¼ cup dairy sour cream
    2 tablespoons mustard sauce or 1 tablespoon
       prepared mustard
    1 tablespoon instant minced onion
       Dash seasoned salt
    8 large crepes

Combine the eggs, ham, cheese, green pepper, pickle, sour cream, mustard, onion and salt. Spread about ¼ cup over each crepe and roll up or fold. Serve the crepes cold or arrange them in a greased baking sheet and heat in a preheated 400°F oven 10 minutes.

Dressy Eggs with Mornay Sauce

This is a form of deviled eggs that combines Thousand Island dressing, Worcestershire sauce and mustard. The recipe makes 4 servings.

6 eggs, hard cooked
1 cup Thousand Island dressing
1 tablespoon Worcestershire sauce
2 teaspoons dry mustard
1 teaspoon celery salt
4 crepes
Mornay Sauce

Chop the eggs finely. In a medium bowl, combine the eggs, dressing, Worcestershire sauce, dry mustard, celery salt. Place about ¼ cup of filling in each crepe. Roll up or fold. Arrange in a shallow baking dish or pan. Spoon the Mornay Sauce over the crepes. Broil until bubbly, about 3 minutes.

Mornay Sauce

2 tablespoons butter
2 tablespoons flour
1 cup milk or cream
1 tablespoon minced onion
1 egg yolk
3 tablespoons Parmesan cheese
Dash cayenne pepper

Melt the butter; stir in the flour and cook until frothy. Add milk or cream, onions; cook and stir over low heat until smooth and thickened. Stir in the egg yolk, Parmesan cheese and cayenne pepper. Cook 1 minute.

Egg Crepes Calcutta

One of the easiest crepe fillings we know, but also one of the best! The recipe makes 8 large crepes, or 4 (2-crepe) servings.

- 1 can (10⅔ ounces) cream of shrimp soup
- 1 teaspoon curry powder
- 6 hard-cooked eggs, chopped
- ½ cup chopped celery
- 1 tablespoon lemon juice
- 8 large crepes

Combine the soup and curry powder and blend. Stir in the eggs, celery and lemon juice. Spread about ⅓ cup of the filling on each crepe. Roll up or fold. Arrange in a greased baking dish or pan and heat in a preheated 350°F oven 20 minutes.

Eggs Benedict

Here is a new version of a glamorous but simple dish.
You will have 6 servings for brunch or lunch.

    6 eggs
      Butter
   12 crepes
    6 slices Canadian bacon or 2 cups, cubed
    2 cups Hollandaise sauce

Poach the eggs until cooked but still soft. Butter 6 individual ramekins. Line each with a crepe, a little Hollandaise sauce, a layer of ham, one egg, another crepe.
Spoon the remaining sauce over the ramekins. Broil
about 6 inches from the heat for 2 to 3 minutes.

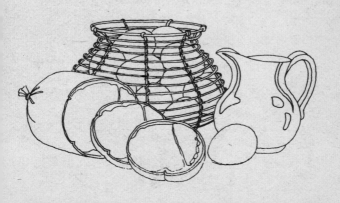

Festive Scrambled Egg Crepes

The smooth cheese sauce is delicious over the creamy eggs — a perfect choice for company. The recipe makes 6 servings.

  6 eggs
  ½ cup evaporated milk
  ½ teaspoon salt
  ¼ teaspoon pepper
  1 package (3 ounces) cream cheese, cubed
  2 tablespoons green onion, sliced
  2 tablespoons butter
 12 crepes
  1 package (1¼ ounces) cheese sauce mix
  2 tablespoons chopped pimiento

Beat together eggs, milk, salt and pepper. Add cream cheese cubes and green onions. Melt the butter in large skillet. Add the egg mixture. Cook, stirring until the eggs are set but still moist. Fill the crepes with about ¼ cup of the egg mixture. Roll up. Prepare the cheese sauce mix according to the package directions; add the pimiento. Spoon the sauce over the crepes to serve.

Souffle in Crepe Cups

These pretty little individual souffles will remind you of popovers. Small crepes work best in this recipe — be sure there are no holes in the crepes or the filling will leak through. This recipe makes 2 dozen souffle cups, or enough for 8 to 12 servings. You may need to borrow a second muffin tin, so you can have 24 cups.

1 can (10½ ounces) cream of asparagus soup
1 cup shredded Cheddar cheese
4 eggs, separated
24 small crepes

In a small saucepan, heat the soup and cheese together until the cheese melts. Beat the egg yolks slightly and add them to the soup-cheese mixture. Beat the whites until stiff but not dry. Gently fold the soup-cheese mixture into the whites. Generously grease 24 muffin cups and fit the crepes in them. Fill each crepe-lined muffin cup almost full of souffle mixture. Bake them in a preheated 325°F oven about 35 to 40 minutes. Serve immediately.

Danish Vegetable Crepes

Serve these crepes as a special side-dish or a unique entree. Fresh cauliflower can be substituted for frozen. The recipe makes 8 small or 4 large crepes.

> 1 package (10 ounces) frozen cauliflower
> 1 can (10¾ ounces) cream of mushroom soup
> ¼ cup finely chopped green pepper
> 2 tablespoons chopped pimiento
> 2 tablespoons sherry
> 4 large or 8 small crepes
> ¼ cup shredded American or Swiss cheese or 2 slices

Cook the cauliflower according to package directions until just barely tender; drain. Combine the cauliflower, soup and all the remaining ingredients except the cheese and crepes. Spoon about ¼ cup of the mixture down center of each large crepe; spoon about 2 tablespoons on each small crepe. Roll up or fold. Arrange in a greased baking dish or pan. Sprinkle with shredded cheese or top with slices of cheese. Bake in a preheated 350°F oven about 15 minutes.

Creamy Green Bean Crepes

This is an up-dated version of an old-favorite—green bean casserole. It is a clever way to serve a vegetable as a side dish or a luncheon entree. The recipe makes 8 servings.

- 1 package (10½ ounces) frozen French-style green beans
- 1 can (10¾ ounces) cream of onion soup
- ½ cup shredded Swiss cheese
- ¼ cup dairy sour cream
- ¼ toasted chopped almonds
- 8 crepes

Cook the beans according to the package directions until just barely tender. Drain. Mix them with the soup, cheese, sour cream and almonds. Spread about ¼ cup of the mixture over each crepe. Roll up or fold. Arrange in a greased baking dish or pan and heat in a preheated 350°F oven 10 to 15 minutes.

Creamy Spinach Surprise

Here is an inexpensive meal that tastes like a million. It is great for family or company. The recipe makes 6 servings.

- 3 packages (10 ounces each) frozen chopped spinach
- 1 package (8 ounces) cream cheese, softened
- 1 pint (2 cups) dairy sour cream
- ¼ cup chopped onion
- ¼ teaspoon nutmeg
- 1 teaspoon salt
- ¼ teaspoon pepper
- 12 hot dogs, cooked
- 12 crepes

Cook the spinach according to the package directions; drain thoroughly. In a medium bowl, combine the spinach, cream cheese, sour cream, onion, nutmeg, salt and pepper; blend well. Fill each crepe with about ¼ cup of the mixture. Place a hot dog in center of each. Roll up or fold. Place seam side down in a greased shallow pan. Cover. Bake in a preheated 350°F oven 20 minutes.

Crepes Florentine

Even spinach-haters go for these rich, cheese-topped crepes. They make an attractive mid-week supper. The recipe makes 6 main-dish servings.

  2 packages (10 ounces each) frozen chopped spinach
  2 tablespoons butter
  2 tablespoons flour
  ½ teaspoon salt
  1 tablespoon instant minced onion
  1 cup milk
  6 large or 12 small crepes
  4 slices American or Swiss cheese

Cook the spinach according to the package directions. Drain, if necessary. In a medium saucepan, melt the butter, blend in the flour, salt and instant onion. Cook and stir over medium high heat until frothy. Add the milk and cook and stir until the mixture comes to a boil and is smooth and thickened. Stir in the spinach. Spoon ½ cup of the filling down the center of each large crepe, spoon ¼ cup down the center of each small crepe. Arrange in a greased baking dish or pan. Top with the cheese slices. Bake in preheated 350°F oven 20 to 25 minutes.

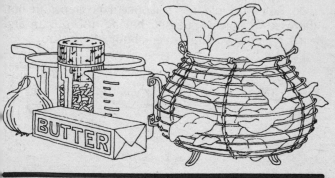

Crepes Ratatouille

Ratatouille is a Mediterranean specialty—a savory combination of vegetables simmered in robust tomato sauce. The recipe makes 8 servings.

    3 tablespoons oil
    1 medium onion, chopped
    1 medium green pepper, chopped
    1 clove garlic, minced
    1 medium eggplant, peeled and diced
    1 medium zucchini, cut in chunks
    1 can (8 ounces) tomato sauce with herbs
    ½ cup water
    1 teaspoon salt
    ½ teaspoon basil or oregano
    8 large or 16 small crepes

Heat the oil in a skillet. Add the onion, green pepper and garlic and cook over medium-high heat until the onion is tender. Add the eggplant, zucchini, tomato sauce, water and seasonings. Heat to boiling, then reduce the heat to simmer. Cover and simmer 15 minutes, then uncover and simmer 15 minutes longer. Spoon about ½ cup of the ratatouille down the center of each large crepe; spoon ¼ cup down the center of each small crepe. Roll up or fold. Serve at once if the crepes are hot, otherwise arrange in greased baking dish or pan and heat in a preheated 350°F oven about 20 minutes.

Garden Crepes

Cook the vegetables until they are just crisp-tender and you will enjoy the most in color, flavor, and vitamins. The recipe makes 6 servings.

> 2 medium zucchini
> 2 teaspoons salt
> 3 tablespoons butter
> 1 medium green pepper, chopped
> 1 small onion, chopped
> 2 medium tomatoes, chopped
> 1 tablespoon chopped fresh dill weed or ½ teaspoon dried dill weed
> 1 cup shredded Cheddar, Swiss or Provolone cheese
> 6 large or 12 small crepes

Grate the zucchini into a mixing bowl and sprinkle with salt. Let it stand 1 hour. Drain, rinse with cold water, then drain thoroughly. Heat the butter in a skillet. Add the vegetables and dill and cook and stir over high heat about 5 minutes or until just tender. Spoon ½ cup of the filling down the center of each large crepe; spoon ¼ cup down the center of each small crepe. Roll up or fold. Arrange on a heat-proof platter, greased baking dish or pan. Sprinkle with the cheese. Broil 6 inches from the heat about 4 to 5 minutes or just until the cheese melts.

Mexican Eggplant Crepes

The flavors are rich, mild and subtle. Just add a crisp salad, fruit for dessert and you have made a memorable meal. The recipe makes 4 to 6 main-dish servings.

¼ cup oil
1 small onion, chopped
1 medium eggplant, peeled and cubed
1 can (8 ounces) tomato sauce
½ cup water
½ cup chopped pitted ripe olives
½ teaspoon salt
¼ teaspoon cumin
1 cup shredded Monterey Jack cheese
8 large or 12 small crepes

Heat the oil in a skillet. Add the onion and cook over medium heat until tender, stirring often. Add the eggplant; cook and stir 2 to 3 minutes. Stir in the tomato sauce, water, olives and seasonings and simmer about 5 minutes. Spoon about ⅓ cup down the center of each large crepe; spoon 3 tablespoons down the center of each small crepe. Roll up or fold and place in a greased baking dish or pan. Spoon any remaining filling over the crepes. Sprinkle with shredded cheese. Bake in a preheated 350°F oven 20 minutes, or heat in a broiler 3 to 4 minutes, or until the cheese melts.

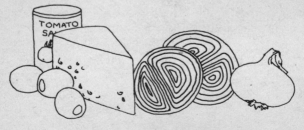

Spinach Souffle Crepe Casserole

One of our favorite recipes, this uses crepes in layers instead of less-than-beautiful crepes. The recipe makes 6 wedges.

    1   pound fresh spinach
    1   package (3 ounces) cream cheese, softened
    3   eggs
    1   cup shredded Mozzarella cheese, divided
    2   tablespoons milk or cream
    ½   teaspoon grated lemon peel
    1   tablespoon lemon juice
    ½   teaspoon basil
    ½   teaspoon onion salt
    ¼   teaspoon pepper
    8   large or 16 small crepes

Wash the spinach well; remove the stems. Using only the water that clings to the leaves, cook just until tender. Drain, if necessary, and chop. Beat together the cream cheese, eggs, ½ cup of the Mozzarella cheese, milk and all the seasonings. Stir in the spinach and mix well. Line a greased 1½ quart casserole or baking dish with 4 crepes. Spoon in half the spinach mixture and cover with 2 crepes. Spread the remaining spinach mixture over the crepes and top with 2 more crepes. Sprinkle with the remaining ½ cup Mozzarella cheese. Bake in a preheated 350°F oven 25 to 30 minutes.

Waldorf Salad Crepes

Crepes with a crunchy, cold filling can be a delightful surprise. Serve these as a salad or side dish to accompany a roast, chops or a steak. You can use Orange Crepes for additional flavor. The recipe makes 6 to 8 crepes of either size.

  3 apples, cored and chopped
  ½ cup sliced celery
  ¼ cup chopped walnuts
  ¼ cup mayonnaise or salad dressing
  1 teaspoon sugar
    Dash salt
  ¼ cup whipping cream, whipped
  6 to 8 leaves leaf lettuce
  6 to 8 crepes

Combine the apples, celery, walnuts, mayonnaise, sugar and salt. Gently fold in whipped cream. Put a lettuce leaf on each crepe, then top it with the apple mixture. Roll up, fastening the crepe with wooden pick if necessary.

Crepes
for Desserts

There is a dessert crepe for every taste and occasion. You will find crepes with fresh fruit, crepes with custard, pudding or ice cream fillings—plus elegant crepe cakes. For a sophisticated after-theater crowd, serve the sinfully rich Brandy Alexander Crepes. For a dramatic finale to a special dinner, serve the famous Crepe Suzettes. And, we have not forgotten the kids— serve them Rocky Road Crepes (using Chocolate Crepes, naturally), or Peanut Butter and Jelly Crepes!

All-American Apple Crepes

The crunch of walnuts and tang of Cheddar cheese make these crepes a challenge to Mom's apple pie. The recipe makes 6 servings.

> 1 can (1 pound 4 ounces) apple pie filling
> ½ cup diced sharp Cheddar cheese
> ½ cup chopped walnuts
> 1 teaspoon grated lemon peel
> 6 large or 12 small crepes
>   Whipped cream or ice cream

Mix together the pie filling, cheese, walnuts and lemon peel. Spoon about ⅓ cup onto the center of each large crepe; spoon a scant 3 tablespoons on each small crepe. Roll up or fold. Arrange the crepes on a greased baking sheet and bake in a preheated 400°F oven 10 minutes. Serve hot or warm, topped with whipped cream or ice cream.

Apricot Crepes

Rich with butter and rum, these golden sauced crepes are a dessert spectacular. Do be sure to flame them! The recipe makes 8 servings of one large or two small crepes.

> 2 cans (1 pound 4 ounces each) apricot
>   halves
> 1 cup (½ pound) butter
> ¼ cup sugar
> ¼ to ½ cup dark rum
>   Dash salt
> 8 large or 16 small crepes
> ⅔ cup orange-flavored liqueur

Drain the apricots, reserving the syrup. Reserve 12 apricot halves. Puree remaining apricot halves and all syrup in blender or food mill. In a large skillet, chafing dish or finishing pan, combine the apricot puree, butter, sugar, rum and salt. Simmer 3 minutes, stirring frequently. Fold the crepes in quarters and add them to the apricot mixture, along with the reserved apricot halves. Stir and cook until the crepes and apricots are hot. In a small saucepan, warm the liqueur. Pour it over the crepes in the pan and ignite. Spoon flaming sauce over the crepes until the flames die down. Serve at once.

Apricot Nutmeg Pudding Crepes

The filling for this dessert is easy and delicious. You will have 16 small crepes-full, enough for 8 generous or 16 regular dessert servings.

- 1 package (3½ ounces) instant vanilla pudding
- ¾ teaspoon nutmeg
- ¼ teaspoon cinnamon
- 1 cup milk
- 1 jar (10 ounces) apricot, peach or pineapple jam
- ½ teaspoon vanilla
- 16 small crepes
  Confectioners' sugar

Stir together the pudding mix, nutmeg, cinnamon and milk. Let the mixture stand until set. Stir in the apricot jam and vanilla. Spread the crepes with the jam-pudding mixture and roll up. Arrange on a serving platter or individual serving plates. Sprinkle with confectioners' sugar.

Banana Cream Crepes

Smooth, rich and wonderful, this recipe makes 6 servings of a single large or small crepe each. Try using Orange or Dessert Crepes for more flavor.

- 3 bananas
- 1 teaspoon grated lemon peel
- 1 tablespoon lemon juice
- 1 cup sour cream
- ½ cup whipping cream
- 2 tablespoons brown sugar
- 6 crepes
- Brown sugar

Slice the bananas into a bowl or dish and sprinkle them with the lemon peel and lemon juice. Whip the cream and fold it into the sour cream along with the 2 tablespoons brown sugar. Divide the banana slices among crepes and roll up or fold. Spoon the cream mixture generously on each crepe, then sprinkle each with small amount of brown sugar.

Brandied Peaches and Cream

An exceptionally pretty dessert, you could serve these crepes at a birthday luncheon instead of cake and ice cream. The recipe makes 12 crepes.

- 1½ cups orange juice
- ⅔ cup molasses
- ½ cup sugar
- 2 tablespoons cornstarch
- 2 tablespoons brandy or 1 teaspoon brandy extract
- 2 cans (1 pound each) sliced peaches, drained
- 12 crepes
  Whipped cream or ice cream

In a large saucepan, combine the orange juice, molasses, sugar and cornstarch. Bring them to a boil; reduce the heat and simmer about 10 to 15 minutes or until thickened. Add the brandy and peaches. Fill each crepe with about ¼ cup of the filling. Fold cornucopia style. Serve with whipped cream or ice cream.

Brandy Alexander Crepes

Rich and sinfully delicious, these sophisticated crepes harmonize perfectly with an after-concert dinner. The recipe makes 12 crepes.

    1 envelope unflavored gelatin
    ¼ cup cold water
    ⅔ cup sugar
       Dash salt
    3 eggs, separated
    ⅓ cup brandy
    ⅓ cup dark creme de cacao
    1 cup whipping cream, whipped
   12 crepes
       Whipped Cream

Sprinkle the gelatin over water in a small saucepan to soften. Stir in ⅓ cup of the sugar, the salt and egg yolks. Cook and stir over low heat until the mixture begins to thicken, about 5 minutes. Remove the pan from the heat; stir in the brandy and creme de cacao. Chill until syrupy, stirring occasionally. Beat the egg whites until soft peaks form. Gradually add the remaining ⅓ cup sugar and beat to stiff peaks. Fold in the gelatin mixture along with the whipped cream. Place about ¼ cup of the filling in the center of each crepe. Fold cornucopia style or as for blintzes. (See Folding Crepes.) Serve with additional whipped cream.

Butterscotch Pear Crepes

With crepes in the freezer and a can of pears on the shelf, you can come up with this fancy dessert in almost no time. The recipe makes 6 servings.

    1   can (1 pound) Bartlett pear halves
    2   teaspoons cornstarch
    ½   cup firmly packaged brown sugar
    2   tablespoons sherry
    2   tablespoons butter
    6   large or 12 small crepes
  1½   pints vanilla ice cream

Drain the pears, reserving the syrup. Combine the cornstarch and brown sugar in a small saucepan. Blend in the reserved pear syrup. Cook and stir it over medium-high heat until the mixture comes to a boil and is smooth and thickened. Stir in the sherry and butter until the butter melts. Dice the pears and stir them into the sauce. Put about ½ cup of ice cream in the center of each crepe and roll up or fold. Spoon the warm pear sauce over the crepes to serve.

California Fruit Crepes

Flavorful nectarines star in a buttery orange sauce and make this crepe combination something special for patio parties. You will have 6 servings from this recipe.

  ¼ cup butter
  2 tablespoons cornstarch
  ¾ cup orange juice
  ½ cup water
  ½ cup firmly-packed brown sugar
  ¼ teaspoon salt
  ¼ teaspoon pumpkin pie spice
  2 large or 3 medium nectarines, sliced
  1 medium banana, sliced
12 small or 6 large crepes

Melt the butter in a saucepan. Blend in the cornstarch and cook and stir over medium heat until bubbly. Stir in the orange juice, water, sugar, salt and spice. Cook and stir until mixture comes to a boil and is smooth and thickened. Stir in the fruits and heat through. Spoon the fruit filling down center of the crepes and fold over to serve, or fold the crepes in quarters and spoon the filling over them.

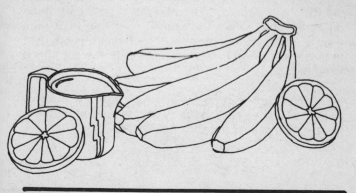

Cherry Crepes Jubilee

Here is a crepe-wrapped version of the famous cherries jubilee dessert. Do flame the crepes for a dessert time spectacular! The recipe makes 8 servings.

- 1 can or jar (1 pound 1 ounce) pitted dark sweet cherries
  Water
- ¼ cup sugar
- 2 tablespoons cornstarch
- 2 tablespoons butter
- 1 teaspoon grated lemon peel
- 1 tablespoon lemon juice
- 1½ pints rich vanilla ice cream
- 8 small crepes
- 2 tablespoons to ¼ cup cherry brandy or liqueur

Drain the cherries, reserving the syrup. Add water to syrup to make 1 cup. In a medium saucepan, stir together the sugar and cornstarch. Blend in the cherry juice and cook and stir over medium-high heat until the mixture comes to a boil and is smooth and thickened. Stir in the butter, lemon peel, lemon juice and cherries; keep warm. (Transfer to chafing dish if desired.) Divide the ice cream into ½ cup portions and center 1 portion on each crepe. Heat the brandy over low heat until warm. Ignite and pour over the cherry mixture. Stir until flames die out, then spoon it over the ice cream filled crepes.

Note: You can wrap crepes around ice cream a day or two in advance; cover with plastic wrap and return to freezer until dessert time.

Chocolate Orange Mousse Crepes

Topped with whipped cream and curls of chocolate, the blend of chocolate and orange flavors make this a fantastic dessert. The recipe makes 6 (2-crepe) servings or 12 single crepes.

   1   package (3½ ounces) chocolate pudding and pie
         filling mix
1½   cups half and half
   ¼   cup orange-flavored liqueur or orange juice
   1   cup whipping cream
   ¼   cup confectioners' sugar
   2   teaspoons grated orange peel
 12   large crepes
         Whipped cream
         Shaved chocolate curls

Cook the pudding mix and half and half over medium heat according to the package directions. When it begins to boil, remove it from the heat and stir in the liqueur. Cover the surface with plastic wrap. Cool thoroughly, but do not refrigerate. Whip the cream until frothy. Gradually beat in the sugar and orange peel until soft peaks form. Fold it into the chocolate mixture. Spoon about ¼ cup of the filling down the center of each crepe. Roll up or fold. Top with additional whipped cream and garnish with chocolate curls.

Chocolate Peanut Crepes

Chocolate Crepes wrap around a peanut filling in this recipe. You top the scrumptious crepes with ice cream or whipped cream. The recipe makes 8 (2-crepe) servings or 16 single crepes.

3   cups finely-chopped peanuts
1⅔ cups confectioners' sugar
¼   cup grated orange peel
½   cup orange juice
16 Chocolate Crepes
    Vanilla ice cream or whipped cream

Stir together the peanuts, sugar, orange peel and orange juice. Spread about 3 to 4 tablespoons of the filling over each crepe. Roll up or fold. Top with ice cream or whipped cream to serve.

Coconut Custard Crepes

You may use any size crepes for this dessert. It is so rich that small servings are in order—at least 10 to 12 servings, in fact, from this recipe.

    3 eggs
    1 cup light corn syrup
    1 can (3½ ounces) flaked coconut
    ¼ cup brown sugar
       Dash salt
    3 tablespoons butter, melted
    1 teaspoon vanilla
   12 crepes

Beat the eggs slightly, then add the corn syrup, coconut, brown sugar, salt, butter and vanilla and mix. Generously butter a 9x13x2-inch or 7x11x2-inch baking dish or pan and pour about ½ cup of coconut mixture into the pan. Spread about 1 tablespoon of the coconut mixture over each crepe and roll them up tightly. Arrange the crepes on the coconut mixture in the pan. Pour any remaining coconut mixture over the crepes. Bake them in a preheated 350°F oven about 25 to 30 minutes or until a knife inserted off center comes out clean.

Crepes Cardinal

The brilliant red double-berry sauce gives this dessert its name. The crepes can be topped with whipped cream, ice cream or sour cream, if you wish. The recipe makes 8 to 12 servings.

- 1 package (10 ounces) frozen raspberries, thawed
- ½ cup water
- ¼ cup sugar
- 2 tablespoons cornstarch
- 1 teaspoon grated lemon peel
- 1 tablespoon lemon juice
- 1 quart fresh strawberries, hulled and sliced
- 8 to 12 crepes

Drain the raspberries, reserving the syrup. Press the berries through a sieve to remove the seeds, then pour ½ cup water over the pulp and seeds remaining in the sieve to rinse out any additional fruit. Combine the sugar and cornstarch in a small saucepan. Add the strained berries. Cook and stir over medium-high heat until the mixture comes to a boil and is smooth and thickened. Remove the pan from the heat and stir in the lemon peel and lemon juice. Cool, then stir in the strawberries. Put a generous tablespoon of sauce in center of each crepe and quarter-fold, fold in half or roll up. Spoon the remaining sauce over the crepes to serve.

Crepes Suzette

Sometimes great things happen by accident. The first time Crepes Suzette were made, the flames were accidental, but now they are part of the excitement and fun of this famous French recipe. The recipe makes 12 crepes.

½ cup sugar
1½ teaspoons grated or thin strips of lemon peel
2 tablespoons lemon juice
1½ teaspoons grated or thin strips of orange peel
¼ cup orange juice
⅓ cup butter
1 ounce maraschino cherry juice
1 ounce Grand Marnier
1 ounce cognac
1 ounce Cointreau
12 crepes

Heat ½ cup of the sugar in a skillet, finishing pan or blazer pan of a chafing dish. Stir until the sugar is carmelized. Add the orange and lemon peels and juices along with the butter; stir until the syrup begins to bubble. Add the maraschino juice, and liqueurs. Add the crepes one at a time. Fold them in half and then in quarters, coating well with the sauce. Ignite. Spoon the liquid over the crepes until the flames die down. Serve at once.

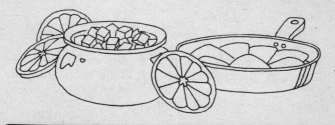

Custard Pear Crepes with Apricot Wine Sauce

A spirited crepe recipe that combines the flavors of pears and apricots, this dessert will impress your guests. The recipe makes 6 (2-crepe) servings or 12 single crepes.

> 1 package (3¾ ounces) instant vanilla pudding and pie filling
> 2 cups cold milk
> ½ teaspoon rum extract
> 1 can (1 pound) sliced pears, drained
> 12 large crepes
> Apricot Wine Sauce

Prepare the pudding mix according to the package directions, using the 2 cups milk and rum extract. Add the pear slices. Cover and chill. Spoon about ¼ cup of the filling down the center of each crepe. Roll up or fold and refrigerate until ready to serve. Serve with flaming Apricot Wine Sauce.

Apricot Wine Sauce

> 2 tablespoons butter
> 2 tablespoons sugar
> ¾ cup apricot jam
> 1 cup port wine
> 3 tablespoons brandy
> 3 tablespoons rum

Heat the butter in a finishing pan, shallow skillet or the blazer pan of a chafing dish. Stir in the sugar and jam; heat to boiling. Add the wine, brandy and rum; warm slightly. Ignite and pour over the crepes.

Danish Raspberry Crepes

Tangy raspberries in a sparkling glaze make these crepes light enough to serve at the end of a large meal, fancy enough to serve for a "dessert only" occasion. The recipe makes 6 servings.

2 packages (10 ounces each) frozen raspberries, thawed
1 cup water
1 package (4¾ ounces) raspberry-currant Danish dessert
2 teaspoons grated lemon peel
2 tablespoons lemon juice
6 large or 12 small crepes
Whipped cream or dairy sour cream

Drain the raspberries, reserving the syrup. In medium saucepan, combine the reserved raspberry syrup, water and Danish dessert. Cook and stir over medium-high heat until the mixture comes to a boil. Boil one minute, stirring constantly. Cool, then stir in the raspberries, lemon peel and juice. Serve warm or cold over rolled or quarter-folded crepes. Top with whipped cream or sour cream.

Date Pudding Crepes

These crepes are rich and chewy and altogether wonderful! The recipe makes 12 to 16 servings.

  2 eggs
½ cup sugar
  2 tablespoons flour
  1 teaspoon baking powder
⅛ teaspoon salt
  2 tablespoons milk
  1 cup diced dates
  1 cup chopped nuts
12 large crepes or 16 small crepes
    Whipped Cream

Beat the eggs until frothy. Gradually add the sugar and beat until thick and lemon colored. Stir together the flour, baking powder and salt; add them to the eggs. Stir in the milk, then mix in the dates and nuts. Fill each small crepe with about 2½ tablespoons of the filling; fill each large crepe with about ¼ cup of the filling. Fold as for blintz. (See Folding crepes.) Place them in a greased shallow baking dish or pan. Bake in a preheated 350°F oven 25 to 30 minutes. Serve with whipped cream.

Double Dutch Apple Crepes

You could use apple or blueberry pie filling for another version of this tasty dessert crepe. The recipe makes 6 servings.

  2 cups applesauce
  1 apple, cored and sliced very thin
  2 tablespoons honey
  1 teaspoon cinnamon
  6 crepes
  ¼ cup butter
  ¼ cup flour
  ¼ cup sugar
  ¼ cup chopped pecans

Mix the applesauce, apple slices, honey and cinnamon and spread over the crepes. Roll or fold and arrange in a greased baking dish or on a greased cookie sheet. Cut the butter, flour and sugar together until they are like coarse crumbs. Stir in the pecans. Sprinkle the crumb mixture over the crepes. Bake in a preheated 400°F oven 10 minutes or until the topping is lightly browned.

Banana Crepes Flambé

Flame these luscious crepes with brandy or banana liqueur for a dramatic dessert. The recipe makes 4 to 6 servings.

¼ cup butter
½ cup brown sugar
1 teaspoon grated lemon peel
12 small crepes
4 bananas, peeled and sliced
1 tablespoon lemon juice
1 tablespoon butter
¼ to ½ cup liqueur or brandy (optional)

Stir the butter, brown sugar and lemon peel together until well blended. Spread about 2 teaspoons over each crepe and fold into quarters. Slice the bananas and sprinkle with lemon juice. Melt the butter in a large skillet or crepe finishing pan. Add the crepes and then top with the bananas. Heat over medium heat or in a chafing dish until hot through. Heat liqueur or brandy, pour over crepes and ignite. Serve the crepes when the flames die out.

Flaming Cherry Crepes

Here is the recipe for a dramatic, sophisticated dessert. The recipe makes 4 (2-crepe) servings.

- 1 can (17 ounces) pitted dark sweet cherries
- ½ cup brandy
- 1 tablespoon cornstarch
- 1 tablespoon water
- 3 tablespoons kirsch
- 8 crepes

Drain the cherries, reserving ½ cup syrup. In a bowl, combine the cherries, reserved syrup and brandy. Cover and refrigerate 3 hours or overnight. Blend the cornstarch and water. In a shallow finishing pan, skillet or the blazer pan of a chafing dish, stir together the cherry mixture and cornstarch-water mixture. Cook and stir over medium heat until thickened. Reduce the heat and add the crepes one at a time, spooning the sauce over them. Quarter-fold the crepes in the syrup. Heat the kirsch in a small saucepan. Ignite and pour it over the crepes.

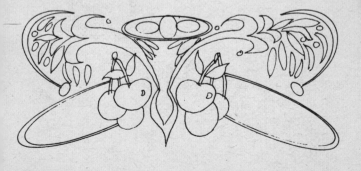

Flaming Pink Pears

Add a bit of drama to your party with these glamorous crepes. The recipe makes 4 to 6 servings, or 3 or 2 crepes each.

    1 can (1 pound 13 ounces) pear halves
    1 package (10 ounces) frozen raspberries, thawed
    2 tablespoons cornstarch
    2 tablespoons sugar
    ½ cup rose' wine
    ¾ cup cognac
    12 small crepes

Drain the pears, reserving ½ cup syrup. Chop the pears. Press the raspberries through a sieve or puree in a blender. In a shallow skillet, finishing pan or blazer pan of a chafing dish, combine the raspberry puree, cornstarch, sugar, reserved pear syrup, wine and ½ cup of the cognac. Stir constantly over medium heat until thickened and clear. Add the crepes one at a time. Fold in half and then in quarters, coating well with sauce. Add the pears. Heat the remaining ¼ cup of cognac, pour it over the pears and ignite. Spoon the liquid over the crepes until the flames die down. Serve immediately.

Flaming Plum Crepes

Even Little Jack Horner would be happy with these fruit-sauced crepes. The recipe makes 6 servings.

- 1 can (17 ounces) purple plums
- 3 tablespoons butter
  - Dash lemon juice
- ¼ cup orange liqueur
- ½ cup brandy
- 1½ pints rich vanilla ice cream
- 6 crepes

Drain the plums, reserving the syrup. Pit and coarsely chop the plums. In a saucepan, combine the plums, syrup, butter and lemon juice. Simmer uncovered 15 minutes, stirring frequently. Stir in the liqueur. Dip the crepes in plum sauce, fold in quarters and arrange in the blazer pan of a chafing dish or finishing pan. Pour half the remaining plum sauce over the crepes, put half in pitcher to pass around. Warm the brandy and pour it over crepes. Ignite. Spoon the flaming sauce over crepes until flames die down. Top the crepes with ice cream and additional plum sauce to serve.

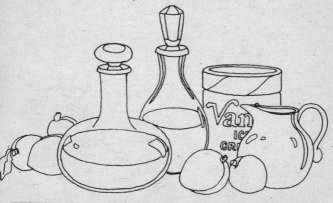

Flaming Strawberry Lime Crepes

Bring out your chafing dish or finishing pan and serve these crepes with a flair. The recipe makes 12 servings.

  1 quart fresh strawberries, hulled and halved
 12 small or large crepes
  ¼ cup butter
  ½ cup brown sugar
  ⅓ cup lime juice
  ½ cup orange liqueur
  1 cup whipped cream, whipped
  1 teaspoon grated lime peel

Arrange about 6 strawberry halves down the center of each crepe. Roll up or fold and set aside. In the blazer pan of a chafing dish or finishing pan, melt the butter. Stir in the sugar, then lime juice. Cook rapidly about 2 minutes. Add the crepes to the pan and spoon the sauce over them, just until hot. Sprinkle the liqueur over the crepes, then ignite. Shake the pan or spoon sauce over the crepes until the flames die down. Top the crepes with whipped cream and lime peel.

Ginger Peachy Crepes

Fresh peaches, sour cream and ginger combine to make this dessert simply elegant. The recipe makes enough for servings of 6 large or 12 small crepes.

4 peaches, peeled and sliced
½ cup brown sugar
½ teaspoon ground ginger
6 large crepes
1 cup dairy sour cream

Sprinkle the sliced peaches with the brown sugar and ginger. Divide the peach slices among the crepes and fold the crepes over the peaches. Spoon the sour cream over the crepes to serve.

Gingered Grape Crepes

Use Thompson seedless green grapes, seeded Tokay or Ribier grapes, the choice is yours. The recipe makes 8 servings.

  2 cups halved seeded or seedless green grapes.
  1 cup dairy sour cream
  ¼ cup brown sugar
  2 to 3 tablespoons minced candied ginger
  8 large or 16 small crepes

Combine the grapes, sour cream, brown sugar and ginger. Spoon about ¼ cup in the center of the large crepes; spoon 2 tablespoons in the center of the small crepes. Roll, fold or fold to form pockets (see Folding Crepes).

Golden Delicious Cream Crepes

Add a dash of cinnamon to the crepe batter for this dessert, or try grated lemon peel. This wonderful recipe makes 6 (2-crepe) servings.

- 4 medium Golden Delicious apples
- ¾ cup sugar
- ¾ cup water
- 2 tablespoons butter
  Dash salt
- 1 package (3 ounces) cream cheese, softened
- ½ cup shredded Cheddar cheese
- ½ cup dairy sour cream
- 12 small crepes

Pare, core and slice the apples. In a saucepan, combine the apple slices, sugar, water, butter and salt. Simmer about 10 minutes or until the apples are tender. Meanwhile, beat the cream cheese and Cheddar cheese together, then blend in the sour cream. Arrange 3 or 4 apple slices on each crepe and top with 1 tablespoon of the cream cheese mixture. Roll up and arrange the crepes in a chafing dish or greased baking pan. Pour the remaining apple syrup over the crepes and heat them in a chafing dish over canned heat or in a preheated 350°F oven for 10 minutes. Top each serving with a spoonful of the remaining cream cheese mixture.

Grasshopper Cream Crepes

Baked in crepe cups, this dessert is picture perfect and refreshing. You could serve it as a late evening dessert after the theater, or as the finale to a formal dinner. The recipe makes 12 servings.

 1 *package (8 ounces) cream cheese*
 1 *package (3 ounces) cream cheese*
 ⅔ *cup sugar*
 2 *eggs*
 ¼ *cup green creme de menthe*
 2 *tablespoons white creme de cacao*
 12 *small crepes*
  Whipped cream
  Chopped pistachio nuts
  Chopped maraschino cherries

Whip the cream cheese until light and fluffy. Beat in the sugar, eggs, creme de menthe and creme de cacao until smooth. Grease 12 muffin cups. Place one crepe in each muffin cup. Fill with the grasshopper filling. Place a sheet of buttered waxed paper lightly on top. Bake in a preheated 300°F oven 20 minutes. Cool. Garnish with whipped cream, pistachio nuts and cherries.

Heavenly Hash Crepes

These unique cold crepes are great for entertaining. You can fill and chill them ahead of time, with no more preparation after that. The recipe makes 9 servings of 1 large crepe each, or 18 servings of 1 small crepe each.

    1 can (11 ounces) mandarin oranges, drained
    1 can (8 ounces) pineapple chunks, drained
    1 jar (8 ounces) maraschino cherries, drained and
      halved
    2 cups miniature marshmallows
    ½ cup whipping cream, whipped
    1 teaspoon grated lemon peel
    ½ cup chopped toasted almonds or pecans
    9 large or 18 small crepes

Combine the fruits, marshmallows, whipped cream, lemon peel and nuts. Cover and chill several hours to blend the flavors and soften the marshmallows. Spoon about ⅓ cup down center of each large crepe; spoon 3 tablespoons down the center of each small crepe. Roll up or fold. Cover and chill until ready to serve.

Hot Fudge Crepes

Even Archie Bunker would go for this mouth-watering crepe dessert. The recipe makes 12 servings.

> 1   can (14 ounces) sweetened condensed milk
> ¼   cup butter
>   Dash salt
> 1   package (6 ounces) semi-sweet chocolate chips
> 1   teaspoon vanilla
> ¼   cup water
> 12   small crepes
> 1½ pints chocolate, coffee or peppermint ice cream

In a saucepan, combine the milk, butter and salt. Heat to boiling and boil 1 minute, stirring constantly. Add the chocolate and vanilla; heat and stir until the chocolate melts. Slowly blend in the water. Keep it warm. Spoon over ¼ cup ice cream onto each crepe and roll up. Spoon the fudge sauce over them to serve. Cover and refrigerate any remaining fudge sauce to use another time.

Note: You can wrap ice cream in the crepes in advance, cover and store in the freezer until dessert time.

Irish Coffee Crepes

The world will beat a path to your door for one of these crepes. Try this filling in Chocolate Crepes. The recipe makes 12 servings.

    1 envelope unflavored gelatin
    ¾ cup sugar
    2 tablespoons instant coffee powder
    1 cup milk
    2 eggs, separated
    2 tablespoons Irish Whiskey or ¼ teaspoon brandy
      extract
    1 carton (9 ounces) frozen non-dairy whipped
      topping, thawed
   12 crepes
      Toasted sliced almonds (optional)

In a saucepan, blend the gelatin, sugar and coffee; gradually add the milk. Cook and stir over low heat until the sugar and gelatin dissolve. Beat the egg yolks. Stir about half the hot mixture into the yolks, then return all to the saucepan. Cook, stirring constantly, about 5 minutes or until slightly thickened. Chill until thickened and syrupy. Add the whiskey and beat until light and frothy. In another bowl, beat the egg whites until stiff; fold them into the gelatin mixture along with the whipped topping. Place about ¼ cup filling in center of crepe. Fold cornucopia style. If desired, serve with extra whipped topping and almonds.

Lemon Cheesecake Crepes

Top these cheesecake crepes with sliced and sweetened nectarines, peaches, plums or berries — sumptuous! The recipe makes 8 servings.

   1 envelope unflavored gelatin
   ¼ cup water
   1 package (3 ounces) cream cheese, softened
   1 cup small curd cottage cheese
   ½ cup sugar
   1 teaspoon grated lemon peel
   3 tablespoons lemon juice
   1 teaspoon vanilla
   ½ cup heavy cream, whipped or 1 cup prepared
       dessert topping
   8 large crepes

Sprinkle the gelatin over the water in a small saucepan. Heat over low heat until the gelatin dissolves. In a blender or with a mixer, beat the dissolved gelatin, cream cheese, cottage cheese, sugar, lemon peel, lemon juice and vanilla until smooth. Chill until the mixture mounds when spooned. Whip the cream and fold into the lemon mixture. Spoon about ⅓ cup of the mixture onto ¼ of each crepe. Fold the sides over to form a triangle, tuck the ends under. Chill for several hours or until the filling is firm.

Lemon Sauced Mincemeat Crepes

Very special for a holiday, these crepes could star at a party or as a dessert. The recipe makes 6 servings.

- 1 cup sugar
- 2 tablespoons cornstarch
- 1 cup boiling water
- 2 teaspoons grated lemon peel
- ¼ cup lemon juice
- 2 tablespoons butter
- 1 cup mincemeat
- 6 crepes

Blend the sugar and cornstarch in a saucepan. Add the boiling water and cook and stir over medium heat until the mixture comes to a boil and is smooth and thickened. Stir in the lemon peel, lemon juice and butter. Keep the sauce warm. Spread the mincemeat over the crepes and roll up. Top with the lemon sauce.

Lemon Yogurt and Strawberry Crepes

A refreshingly simple recipe, these lemon and strawberry crepes are perfect for luncheons or for light desserts. The recipe makes 6 (2-crepe) servings or 12 single-crepe servings.

> 2 pints strawberries, hulled and sliced
> ¾ cup firmly-packed light brown sugar
> ½ teaspoon ground nutmeg
> 2 cartons (8 ounces each) lemon yogurt
> 12 crepes

Combine the strawberries, brown sugar and nutmeg. Cover and let them stand for at least 2 hours. Stir together the yogurt and 2 cups of the strawberry mixture. Spoon about ¼ cup of the strawberry filling in each crepe. Fold the sides over or fold cornucopia style. Top with the remaining strawberry sauce.

Melba Crepes Gateau

Instead of folding crepes around a filling, you stack them to make an impressive towering "cake." This recipe makes 6 servings. If you have a crowd for dessert, just double the recipe and make 2 gateaux.

> 1 package (10 ounces) frozen raspberries, thawed
> 1 tablespoon sugar
> 1 tablespoon cornstarch
> 1 teaspoon lemon juice
> 1 cup whipping cream
> 2 tablespoons sugar
> ½ teaspoon vanilla
> 3 to 4 fresh peaches, peeled and sliced or 1 can (1 pound 13 ounces) cling peach slices, drained
> 6 crepes

Drain the raspberries, reserving the syrup. In a small saucepan, blend the sugar and cornstarch. Stir in the raspberry syrup and cook and stir over medium-high heat until the mixture comes to a boil and is smooth and thickened. Remove it from the heat and stir in the lemon juice. Whip the cream with sugar and vanilla until stiff. Arrange 4 to 5 peach slices in pinwheel fashion on one crepe on a serving plate. Spoon a generous tablespoon of whipped cream between the peach slices. Top with another crepe and repeat the arrangement of peach slices and whipped cream. Repeat until all the crepes, peaches and cream have been layered. Spoon the raspberry sauce over it to serve. Cut the cake in wedges to serve (an electric knife makes cutting easier).

Nectarine Crepes

Fresh nectarines are one of the nicest things about summer, and this nectarine sauce celebrates summer properly. This recipe makes 6 servings.

    2 packages (3 ounces each) cream cheese, softened
    ⅓ cup sugar
    ¼ cup dairy sour cream
    2 teaspoons grated orange peel
    ¼ teaspoon salt
    ¼ teaspoon almond extract
    3 medium nectarines
    ½ cup sugar
    3 tablespoons orange liqueur
       Dash salt
    6 large or 12 small crepes

Beat together the cream cheese, ⅓ cup sugar, sour cream, orange peel, ¼ teaspoon salt and almond extract. Set the mixture aside. Slice two of the nectarines and mash or blend in blender with the sugar, orange liqueur and salt. Slice the remaining nectarine and stir it into the mashed or blended fruit mixture. Spread 1 generous tablespoon of the cream cheese mixture onto each large crepe; spread 2 teaspoons onto each small crepe. Roll up and put 1 large or 2 small crepes on individual serving plates, or arrange on a pretty platter. Spoon the nectarine sauce over the crepes to serve.

Note: If you wish, you may arrange filled crepes in a greased baking dish or pan and heat in a preheated 350°F oven about 15 minutes. While the crepes are heating, heat nectarine sauce in saucepan to spoon over cheese-filled crepes.

Peach-Berry Crepes

Another version of the famous Melba flavors, these crepes are easy to make ahead of time. Just add peaches before serving. The recipe makes 6 servings.

6   large or 12 small crepes
½   cup raspberry jam
6   scoops vanilla ice cream
2½ cups fresh or frozen sliced peaches, thawed and
    drained

Spread the crepes with jam and fold in quarters. Top 1 large or 2 small crepes with a scoop of ice cream. Spoon the peaches over the crepes to serve.

Peanut Butter and Jelly Crepes

Peanut Butter and Jelly Crepes make a great kids' breakfast, a unique brunch feature or a surprisingly good dessert. The recipe makes 6 to 12 servings.

⅓ cup soft butter
⅓ cup creamy or chunk-style peanut butter
⅓ cup jelly or jam
6 large or 12 small crepes
½ cup chopped salted peanuts (optional)

Cream the butter and peanut butter together, then spread about 2 tablespoons on each large crepe, 1 tablespoon on each small crepe. Spread the same amount of jelly on each crepe. Serve cold, or arrange the crepes in a greased baking dish and heat in a preheated 350°F oven 10 to 15 minutes. Sprinkle with chopped peanuts, if desired.

Peanut Gateau

Fluffy peanut and cream filling between crepe layers makes this an impressive "cake." The recipe makes 5 servings.

    1 package (3 ounces) cream cheese, softened
    1 cup confectioners' sugar
    ⅓ cup peanut butter
    1 package (2⅛ ounces) whipped topping mix
    ½ cup cold milk
    1 teaspoon vanilla extract
   10 crepes
      Shaved chocolate curls

Whip cream cheese until soft. Beat in peanut butter. Add the sugar and beat until light and fluffy. Prepare the topping mix with milk and vanilla according to the package directions. Fold the whipped topping into the peanut butter mixture. Spread about 3 tablespoons of the filling on each crepe. Stack the crepes. Garnish the top with chocolate curls. Lightly cover and chill until dessert time. To serve cut into 6 wedges.

Pecan Crepelets

Small crepes can be tucked into muffin cups to make tarts. Be sure that the crepes have no holes in them. If you can make only large crepes, you will have to trim about an inch off all the way around. The recipe makes 6 crepelets.

6 small crepes
2 eggs
½ cup sugar
½ cup dark corn syrup
3 tablespoons butter, melted
1 teaspoon vanilla
¼ teaspoon salt
¾ cup chopped pecans

Butter 6 muffin cups and ease the crepes into the cups. Beat the eggs slightly, then beat in the sugar, corn syrup, butter, vanilla and salt. Divide the pecans among the crepes in the muffin tins, then pour in the sugar-egg mixture. Bake them in a preheated 350°F oven 25 to 30 minutes.

Plum Crepes with Spiced Cream

Pick red, purple or Italian plums for this dessert, or try nectarines, apricots or peaches. The recipe makes 6 servings.

6 *large or 12 small fresh plums, sliced*
3 *tablespoons sugar*
6 *crepes*
1 *cup whipping cream*
¼ *cup confectioners' sugar*
1 *teaspoon vanilla*
½ *teaspoon pumpkin pie spice*

Toss the plum slices and sugar to mix. Divide the plums among the crepes and fold them in half, quarter-fold or roll up. Whip the cream until almost stiff, then add the sugar, vanilla and spice and whip until stiff. Spoon the spiced cream over the fruit-filled crepes.

Praline Crepes

Rich, nutty syrup tops these ice cream-filled crepes. Choose chocolate, vanilla, butter pecan or your favorite ice cream to go in the crepes.

    2   tablespoons butter
    ½   to 1 cup coarsely chopped pecans
    1   cup dark corn syrup
    ½   cup brown sugar
    1   teaspoon vanilla
    1½   to 2 pints ice cream
    6   to 8 large or 12 to 16 small crepes

Melt the butter in a skillet. Add the pecans and cook and stir over medium-high heat until the pecans are lightly browned. Add the syrup, brown sugar and vanilla and heat to boiling, stirring constantly. Boil 1 minute. Cool slightly. Spoon or scoop about ½ cup ice cream onto the center of each large crepe; spoon ¼ cup onto the center of each small crepe. Fold like blintzes, fold over or roll up. Spoon warm or cooled pecan sauce over the crepes to serve.

Pumpkin Cheesecake Crepes

These dainty little cheesecakes bake in individual crepe cups. The recipe makes 16 crepe cups.

   1 package (8 ounces) cream cheese
   ¾ cup sugar
   2 teaspoons cinnamon
   1 teaspoon ginger
   ¼ teaspoon cloves
   2 eggs
   1 can (1 pound) pumpkin
   1 cup chopped pecans
  16 small crepes
     Sweetened dairy sour cream or whipped cream

Beat together the cream cheese, sugar, cinnamon, ginger and cloves until smooth. Beat in the eggs and then the pumpkin and nuts. Place one crepe in each of 16 muffin cups. Fill each with about 3 tablespoons filling. Place a sheet of aluminum foil loosely on top. Bake in a preheated 325°F oven about 20 to 25 minutes or until the centers are firm. Chill the crepes in the pans; then remove. Serve with a dollop of sweetened sour cream or whipped cream.

Raisin Apple Crepes

Canned pie filling gives you a head start on 6 to 12 delicious dessert crepes that taste like French apple pie.

  2 cans (1 pound each) apple pie filling
  1 cup raisins
  1 cup chopped pecans
 ½ teaspoon ground cinnamon
 ½ teaspoon ground nutmeg
12 large crepes
  1 cup dairy sour cream
  2 tablespoons brown sugar
 ½ teaspoon ground nutmeg

Stir together the apple pie filling, raisins, pecans, cinnamon, and nutmeg. Spoon about ¼ cup of the filling down the center of each crepe. Fold in half or quarter-fold. Heat in a preheated 400°F oven 10 minutes. Stir together the sour cream, brown sugar and nutmeg. Spoon the topping over the hot crepes.

Raisin Cream Crepe Gateau

Twelve layers of crepes stacked with vanilla, chocolate and strawberry filling create a beautiful dessert. An electric knife makes cutting this crepe cake easy. If you plan to make it ahead, be sure to cover it well with plastic wrap and chill. The recipe makes 8 to 12 servings.

1	cup raisins
1½	cups butter, softened
4	egg yolks
1½	cups confectioners' sugar
1	teaspoon vanilla
1	ounce unsweetened chocolate, melted
1	teaspoon strawberry flavoring or cheri-suisse liqueur
12	large or small crepes

Grind the raisins, using the coarse blade of a grinder, or freeze and chop them coarsely in a blender. Beat the butter and egg yolks until light and fluffy. Gradually add the sugar. Stir in the raisins. Divide the mixture among 3 small bowls. Stir the vanilla into the mixture in one bowl, the chocolate into the second bowl, and strawberry into the third bowl. Put a crepe on a serving plate and spread it with the vanilla mixture. Top with another crepe and spread it with the chocolate mixture. Top with another crepe and spread it with the strawberry mixture. Repeat until all the crepes have been stacked and spread.

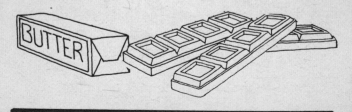

Rocky Road Crepes

Mint, marshmallows and chocolate make this dessert irresistible. The recipe makes 12 single crepe servings, 6 (2-crepe) servings.

  ½ cup butter
  ¾ cup sugar
  2 squares (1 ounce each) unsweetened chocolate, melted
  ½ teaspoon vanilla
  ¼ teaspoon mint extract
  2 eggs
  1 cup miniature marshmallows
 12 crepes
  1 cup whipped cream
  ¼ cup chopped maraschino cherries

Cream the butter until light. Add the sugar and continue beating until fluffy. Blend in melted chocolate, vanilla and mint. Add the eggs, one at a time, beating 5 minutes after each addition. Stir in the miniature marshmallows. Fill each crepe with a scant 3 tablespoons of filling. Fold them into cornucopia shapes. (See Folding Crepes.) Cover and chill. Top with whipped cream and chopped cherries.

Rolled Crepe Cookies

Thin, lacy crepes are best to make these cookies. You can use leftover crepes, or make some special. Rolled Crepe Cookies are elegant with ice cream, sherbet, puddings, and fresh fruit. Make as many cookies as you want.

> *Thin crepes*
> *Melted butter*
> *Sugar*

Brush one side of the crepes lightly with the melted butter and sprinkle lightly with sugar. Roll up tightly and arrange, seam side down, on lightly greased cookie sheet. Bake in a preheated 350°F oven about 10 minutes or until browned and crisp.

Spiced Custard Crepes

A simple custard, plus whipped cream and crepes, makes a dessert to rival France's fanciest. The recipe makes 6 large or 12 small crepes.

  3 eggs
  ½ cup sugar
  1 cup milk
  ¼ teaspoon each ground ginger, mace and cinnamon
  1 teaspoon vanilla
  1 cup whipping cream
     Cinnamon
  6 large or 12 small crepes

Beat the eggs and sugar together in a heavy saucepan. Add the milk and spices. Cook and stir over medium-low heat until the mixture thickens slightly and will coat a metal spoon. DO NOT BOIL. Remove the pan from the heat, stir in the vanilla. Cover the surface of the custard with waxed paper or plastic wrap and chill. Whip the cream and fold half the whipped cream into the custard mixture. Spoon about ¼ cup down the center of each large crepe; spoon 2 tablespoons down the center of each small crepe. Roll up or fold and arrange them on a platter or individual dessert plates. Spoon the remaining custard over the crepes. Top with the remaining whipped cream and sprinkle with additional cinnamon.

Spiced Peach Crepes

A dessert to please everyone, from toddlers to great-grandparents. And, it is very simple to fix. The recipe makes 6 servings.

    1 can (1 pound) sliced cling peaches
    1 tablespoon cornstarch
    1 tablespoon honey
    ¼ teaspoon cinnamon
    1 tablespoon lemon juice
    1 cup cottage cheese
    3 tablespoons honey
    ½ teaspoon cinnamon
    ½ teaspoon grated lemon peel
    6 large or small crepes

Drain the peaches, reserving the syrup. In small sauce-pan, blend the syrup, cornstarch, 1 tablespoon honey and ¼ teaspoon cinnamon. Cook and stir over medium high heat until the mixture comes to a boil and is smooth and thickened. Stir in the lemon juice and peaches; keep warm. Stir together the cottage cheese, 3 tablespoons honey, ½ teaspoon cinnamon and lemon peel. Spread 1 tablespoon of the cheese mixture over each crepe. Roll up. Serve the crepes with warm peach sauce.

Spice Trader Peach Crepes

Ice cream and a unique blend of spices make these easy-to-fix crepes a popular dessert. The recipe makes 6 servings.

1 can (1 pound) cling peach slices
1 tablespoon minced candied ginger
2 sticks cinnamon
8 whole allspice
6 whole cloves
4 cardamon (optional)
1½ pints ice cream
6 crepes

Drain the peaches, reserving the syrup. In a small saucepan, combine the syrup, candied ginger and spices. Heat to boiling, then lower the heat and simmer 15 minutes. Dice the peaches; stir them into syrup and chill. Put about ½ cup ice cream on each crepe and fold or roll up. Spoon the peach syrup over the crepes to serve.

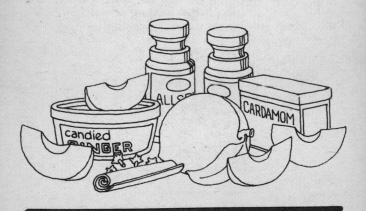

Springtime Crepes Brulee

A rich cream mixture envelops strawberry-filled crepes and is topped by caramelized brown sugar for a superb dessert. The recipe makes 8 servings.

2   pints fresh strawberries, hulled and sliced
½   cup sugar
8   large crepes or 16 small crepes
1   package (8 ounces) cream cheese, softened
1½ cups dairy sour cream
½   cup sugar
1   teaspoon grated lemon peel or vanilla
1   cup firmly-packed brown sugar

Sprinkle the strawberries with the ½ cup sugar. Divide the strawberries among the crepes and fold or roll up. Arrange the crepes in a greased baking dish or pan. Beat together the cream cheese, sour cream, the second ½ cup sugar and lemon peel or vanilla. Spread the cream cheese mixture over the crepes. Sprinkle with brown sugar. Broil at least 6 inches from the heat for just a few minutes or until the sugar bubbles.

Strawberry Crepes de la Creme

Serve these elegant crepes at a buffet or as a special dessert. The recipe makes 16 servings.

- 2 pints fresh strawberries hulled and sliced
- ⅓ cup sugar
- 1 package (8 ounces) cream cheese, softened
- 1 cup confectioners' sugar
- 2 tablespoons rum or orange-flavored liqueur
- 16 crepes

Sprinkle the ⅓ cup sugar over the strawberries; set them aside at least one hour. Beat the cream cheese and confectioners' sugar together until light and fluffy. Stir in the rum and 2 cups of the sweetened strawberries. Fill each crepe with a scant ¼ cup of filling. Roll up or fold. Spoon the reserved strawberries on top.

Note: For variations, you can add the following to the basic crepe batter: 1 teaspoon sugar, 1 tablespoon rum or orange liqueur, and ¼ teaspoon ground nutmeg.

Strawberry Crepes with Devonshire Cream

Sour cream plus whipping cream make this American version of Britain's famous rich topping. The recipe makes 8 servings.

  1 envelope unflavored gelatin
  ¾ cup cold water
  ½ cup sugar
  1 cup dairy sour cream
  1 teaspoon vanilla
  1 cup whipping cream, whipped
  8 large crepes
  2 pints fresh strawberries, hulled and sliced

Sprinkle the gelatin over cold water in a saucepan to soften. Heat over very low heat until the gelatin dissolves. Stir in the sugar until it dissolves, then blend in the sour cream and vanilla. Fold in the whipped cream and chill until the mixture mounds when spooned. Spread about ½ cup of the cream mixture down the center of each crepe. Fold each side of the crepe over the filling. Spoon sliced strawberries over the crepes to serve.

Tropical Crepes

Smooth and rich, these buttery fruit crepes are a nice finale to a special meal. The recipe makes 12 crepes.

½ cup sweet butter
1 cup confectioners' sugar
1 tablespoon cognac
1 tablespoon lemon juice
½ cup drained crushed pineapple
½ cup mashed banana
3 tablespoons finely-chopped crystallized ginger
12 small Dessert Crepes

Whip the butter with the sugar until light and fluffy. Beat in the cognac, lemon juice; and the pineapple, banana and ginger. Divide the butter mixture among crepes. Roll up.

Note: For a variation, add 1 cup chopped mixed candied fruit in place of pineapple and banana.

Index